AFTER THE
SHOOTING STOPS

AFTER THE
SHOOTING STOPS

THE AFTERMATH OF WAR

KATHLYN GAY AND MARTIN GAY

TWENTY-FIRST CENTURY BOOKS
BROOKFIELD, CONNECTICUT

Photographs courtesy of Corbis-Bettmann: p. 12; Corbis: pp. 24, 68; The Granger Collection: p. 36; Brown Brothers: pp. 46, 58; UPI/Corbis-Bettmann: p. 80; Reuters/Corbis-Bettmann: p. 92; Anthony Suau/Gamma Liaison: p. 104.

Library of Congress Cataloging-in-Publication Data

Gay, Kathlyn.
After the shooting stops : the aftermath of war / Kathlyn Gay and Martin Gay.
p.   cm
Includes bibliographical references and index.
Summary: Discusses the major social, political, and technological changes
that occured in the United States as a result of various wars from the
Revolution to the Gulf War.
ISBN 0-7613-3006-2 (lib. bdg.)
1. United States—History, Military—Juvenile literature. 2. War and society—United States—Juvenile literature. [1. United States—History, Military. 2. War and
society.] I. Gay, Martin, 1950–   . II. Title.
E181.G29   1998
355'.00973—dc21   98-11387
                                                              CIP
                                                              AC

Twenty-First Century Books
A Division of The Millbrook Press, Inc.
2 Old New Milford Road
Brookfield, Connecticut 06804

CONTENTS

AFTER THE
SHOOTING STOPS

INTRODUCTION

Wars are a major part of the relatively short history of the United States. These wars have been fought for a variety of reasons—some of them noble, some ignoble. The United States became a nation as a result of a revolutionary war for independence from Great Britain. Other wars were fought to gain territory, to fulfill what was called the United States' "manifest destiny" to rule the continent. Some wars were initiated because of imperialist tendencies, while others were efforts to establish democracies in various parts of the world. The United States participated in two devastating world wars, but one of the worst armed conflicts was a civil war that threatened to destroy the nation.

War stories and memoirs fill the pages of thousands of books. War is the subject of countless movies and TV documentaries. America's wars and those who died in them are memorialized by monuments and statues, and anniversaries mark major battles and the ends of wars.

But what about the aftermath of war? What happened

after the shooting stopped? How did wars change the United States? What efforts have been made throughout the decades to live peacefully? These are some of the questions discussed in this book.

After the American Revolutionary War, the former British colonies had to build a new nation, write a constitution, and deal with money problems. The United States also had to establish itself among the world powers. But these tasks were interrupted by another war with Great Britain, the War of 1812, which ended with a great loss of lives and money, and little if any gain for the United States.

After the War of 1812, however, there were four decades of remarkable economic, technological, and geographic growth. Yet that growth came at a price, as is shown in Chapter 3. Wars were fought during the 1800s with Native Americans and Mexicans over territory, and thousands were maimed or killed. In many parts of the new nation and its western territories, those not directly involved in armed conflict lived with the constant threat of violence.

The United States was less than a century old when the Civil War erupted, leaving more than 600,000 dead. After that four-year war, there was a period of reconstruction, which is covered in Chapter 4. But it was not a peaceful time. Brutal conflicts and killings took place over racial issues and freed slaves' attempts to pursue the dream of equality.

In 1898 still another war broke out, the Spanish-American War. The United States won this "splendid little war," as it was called, and acquired former Spanish possessions that included Cuba, Puerto Rico, and the Philippines. But many Filipinos did not want to be part of the United States and fought a guerrilla war that lasted three years, until 1902.

By that time, various reform groups in the United States were campaigning to make the country a more humane place to live and work. But some of those efforts were put on hold while the United States fought World War I. The aftermath of that war, which was supposed to be the "war to end all wars," actually led to another world conflict, World War II. That war still affects people today who live in the shadow of sophisticated nuclear arms. Some of the experiences of people living in a shell-shocked society are included in Chapter 8.

The Cold War—so called because it was a period of intense rivalry between Communist and non-Communist nations but involved no widespread armed combat—began soon after World War II and lasted into the early 1990s. During this time of instability, the United States fought against communism in other countries' wars—the Korean War in the 1950s and the Vietnam War in the 1960s and 1970s. Later, Americans under the auspices of the United Nations fought against Iraqi aggression in the Persian Gulf War.

Clearly, even though shooting stops for a time, the changes and advancements in the aftermath of war do not seem to lead to a lasting peace. Therefore, nonviolent conflict resolution should be a top priority. As former President Jimmy Carter has pointed out, "Peace is everyone's job."

This early Revolutionary War flag with stars in a circle
was raised over Fort Ticonderoga when patriots seized
the British post in May 1775.

1

AFTER THE REVOLUTION

"The war was over, and it was time that I should look to some other profession than that of arms," Francis H. Brooke wrote in a narrative for his family years after the American Revolutionary War ended in September 1783. Brooke noted that he "was not quite twenty years of age," when the shooting stopped, and "like other young men of the time, having an indulgent father, who permitted me to keep horses, I wasted two or three years in fox-hunting, and sometimes in racing."[1]

Brooke, however, was hardly typical of most Revolutionary War veterans. In fact, some soldiers, like Jeremiah Greenman, were not free to go home until months after the peace treaty was signed.

Greenman had enlisted in the Rhode Island regiment in 1775, when he was just seventeen years old, and had served in numerous campaigns, eventually becoming an officer. During his last assignment at Saratoga, New York, he along with the other soldiers waited through October and November for discharge orders. Greenman reported in a journal that his men were "in a Miserable condition some of [them] not a Shoe or a Stocking to their feet." Although there were attempts to get clothing and shoes for the men, each soldier received "only a pair of Shoes." The discharge order finally arrived on December 5, and that "order had laid in the post office at Albany sinc [*sic*] 18th of Novr." By the morning of December 25, Greenman noted, "all our men had their discharges, [and] in the evening set off with the Bagage [*sic*]."[2]

At home, veterans like Greenman, along with many other former colonists who had never been in the military, faced the difficult process of building a new nation based on the principles of the Declaration of Independence. That document, which spelled out the reasons the British colonies should be free and independent states, had been approved on July 4, 1776, by the Second Continental Congress—a gathering of elected delegates from the colonies.

After eight years of armed conflict, which began before the formal declaration of independence, the new nation faced numerous economic, social, and political challenges. One of the most controversial issues was how to frame a constitution for the United States. Each state had its own constitution and government, but the states were not yet united by a national government. They were linked only by a loose alliance under the Articles of Confederation.

ARTICLES OF CONFEDERATION

In 1776 a committee of thirteen men appointed by the Continental Congress drafted the Articles of Confederation, which was ratified, or formally approved, by the states and became effective March 1, 1781. It provided for a "perpetual Union between the States of New Hampshire, Massachusetts bay, Rhode Island and Providence Plantations, Connecticut, New

York, New Jersey, Pennsylvania, Delaware, Maryland, Virginia, North Carolina, South Carolina and Georgia." But it was a loose confederation with limited powers. There was no judicial branch (federal court system) and no provision had yet been made for a strong executive (president).

Under the Articles, each state remained sovereign, with an independent government, and was allowed one vote in the congress. The new institution was responsible for carrying on foreign affairs such as making treaties and declaring war. It could also settle disputes between states, manage a postal service, establish the value of money, and oversee Indian affairs. However, it shared with the states the power to regulate trade between states and to coin money. The congress could not raise an army, but could help coordinate the operations of the states' militias.

The Articles provided no means for the confederation congress to tax citizens for money to operate the government. It could only ask the states to contribute funds. In 1782, for example, the congress appealed for $10 million to carry on the war and pay for other expenses, but the states supplied only $1.5 million.[3]

One way the confederation raised money was through an agreement with the states to deed land that they claimed in western areas to the federal government. Portions then could be sold to finance government operations.

In one agreement, known as the Northwest Ordinance of 1787, land in the Northwest Territory, north and west of the Ohio River, was turned over to the federal government. The ordinance also established that between three and five states would be formed from the Northwest Territory. A prospective state had to have sixty thousand free inhabitants before it could declare statehood and join the union, and slavery was to be banned in any new state formed in the territory.

Land sales did not ease money problems, however. During the 1780s, the congress continually struggled to raise funds from state legislatures to pay expenses and war debts. It also needed funds to deal with governments of other nations and to protect American interests overseas. Lacking the finances to carry out its duties, the congress had no choice but to print its own paper bills, which soon became almost worthless.

Financial difficulties were also complicated by the fact that each state issued its own paper money, so a dollar in New York, for example, was not worth the same as a dollar in Pennsylvania. Creditors (those who made loans) began to accept only gold and silver for repayment of debts.

Adding to the financial problems was the attitude of European countries. They refused to take the new nation seriously and set up barriers to shipping and trade. As trade and shipping income declined in the United States, the nation's foreign and domestic debt soared.

A major economic depression set in, and from 1784 to 1789 prices of goods, which had been inflated during the war, steadily fell. Farmers were particularly hard hit by the depression. They had enjoyed prosperous times during the war and had mortgaged their farms—borrowed money using their property as security for repayment. The loans enabled them to make improvements or buy more land. But when the prices of their crops declined, farmers could no longer pay their debts. Many were faced with mortgage foreclosures; creditors could legally take over property for unpaid loans.

In various states, farmers and other debtors protested the foreclosures. They also objected to high taxes and laws and court decisions that were unfair to working people, such as jailing debtors because they could not pay their bills. In just one year, 1784, "there were 2000 suits for debt in Worcester County."[4] in western Massachusetts.

UPRISINGS

Over the next two years farmers and other debtors staged numerous protests against unjust legal practices and the lack of a stable monetary system. Beginning in August 1786, Daniel Shays, a captain in the Revolutionary War, led a Massachusetts group in uprisings known as Shays's Rebellion. To prevent the trials and imprisonment of debtors, Shays and his followers closed down the court in Northampton on August 31. A month later rebels stormed the state supreme court in Springfield, but they were driven off by state militia troops. Then in January 1787 Shays and more than one thousand men planned to attack the federal arsenal at Springfield, but again the militia drove the protesters away. Some of them, including Shays, escaped to Vermont.

During this turbulent time, Thomas Jefferson, who was a member of the Continental Congress (later elected the third president of the United States), to some extent supported the rebel actions. He believed people should be able to voice their grievances, and in late January 1787 he wrote a letter to his fellow congressman James Madison (who became the fourth U.S. president) declaring that "a little rebellion now and then is a good thing . . . a medicine necessary for the sound health of government."[5]

Most of the rebels were captured in February 1787. The leaders were tried and convicted of treason, but they were pardoned by the governor of Massachusetts. Shays was not only pardoned but was also eligible for a pension for his Revolutionary War service. However, funds were needed to pay pensions, and there was little to spare, so pensions were not forthcoming until 1818, when the Pension Act was passed by a new federal government.

A NEEDY VETERAN

Although some Revolutionary War veterans finally received allotments, only those who could show real financial need were given pensions. One destitute veteran was Jehu Grant, a former slave owned by a man who sympathized and worked for the British during the war. Grant had feared he would be forced to serve on a British ship, so he escaped to enlist on the American side.

After the war, Grant gained his freedom with the help of Joshua Swan of Connecticut. Swan purchased Grant with the understanding that he would be released from slavery after serving Swan for a time. In his late years, Grant applied for a pension, but he was informed that his claim was invalid because he was a fugitive slave. But he did not let the matter rest. Unable to read or write, Grant dictated a letter in 1836 to the commissioner of pensions, explaining his fear of the British and the considerations that

> induced me to enlist into the American army, where I served faithful about ten months, when my master found and took me home. Had I been taught to read or understand the precepts of the Gospel, "Servants obey your masters," I might have done otherwise, notwithstanding the songs of liberty that saluted my ear, thrilled through my heart. But feeling conscious that I have since compensated my master for the injury he sustained by my enlisting, and that God has forgiven me for so doing and that I served my country faithfully, and they having enjoyed the benefits of my service . . . I cannot but feel it becoming . . . to review my declaration.[6]

The logic of Grant's plea made little difference. He never received a pension.

The poor economic conditions of the 1780s and disputes between states prompted many citizens of the new nation to call for a stronger central government. One of the most persuasive voices was Alexander Hamilton, an advisor to General George Washington during the Revolutionary War. Hamilton was a delegate to a 1786 convention in Annapolis, Maryland, which was called to consider problems between states, among them the regulation of trade.

Hamilton urged his fellow delegates to think "continentally"—to adopt a national, not just a state, view of problems and goals. He helped persuade the gathering to hold another convention the following year in Philadelphia, Pennsylvania, to create a more effective union of states by revising the Articles of Confederation.

The Philadelphia meeting, which became known as the Constitutional Convention, opened in May 1787. Over the next four months delegates from all states except Rhode Island drafted amendments to the articles. But the delegates found that the revisions were unworkable, so they considered a number of plans for a new form of government.

One of the most important issues was how states would be fairly represented in a United States government. Arguments focused on such questions as: should there be one or two houses in the new Congress? Should representation be based on a state's population or should there be equal votes for each state?

After more than a month of debate, the conflict was resolved with a simple plan known as the Great Compromise. It called for two houses of Congress: the upper house, or Senate, and the lower house, or House of Representatives. Each member of the lower house would represent a proportion of the population in his state and would be elected by eligible male voters. Each state would have the same number of senators in the upper house, the Senate, to be elected by state legislatures. Not until 1913, with the ratification of the Seventeenth Amendment, were senators elected directly by the people.

Other compromises focused on slavery. Southern states wanted slaves included in the population count, thus increasing the number of representatives those states could send to the House. However, if slaves were counted, owners would be subject to increased property taxes since slaves were considered property. Thus, slave states agreed that five slaves would be equal to three free men in determining representation. The "three-fifths" compromise also applied for tax purposes.

The constitution strengthened the new government, granting authority to establish courts and make and enforce the supreme laws of the land. Other provisions included the power to collect taxes, borrow money, regulate trade with other nations and Indian tribes, and to raise and support armies and a navy.[7]

The convention realized the need to balance power and spread duties and authority between three branches of government: legislative (the Congress, made up of the House and Senate), executive (the president and other administrative officers), and judiciary (the federal court system). The power of each branch could be checked by the others.

For example, the president has the authority to appoint various administrators and to make treaties, but the Senate must approve these decisions. Congress has the power to enact laws, but the president can veto them. Courts can interpret federal laws and determine whether laws are based on the Constitution, but Congress can impeach judges who are found guilty of illegal acts.

Thirty-nine delegates signed the constitution and sent it to the states for ratification. Only nine states had to approve, a wise provision that prevented a few states from blocking the decision of the majority. Yet ratification was not a simple matter, since each state had to hold a special convention and vote on whether to approve the constitution.

One major concern was the failure of the constitution to spell out individual rights, such as those included in state constitutions. A bill of rights was eventually added, but initially, arguments for and against ratification were debated hotly in the states. Those for a strong central government took over the name "federalists," which had previously been the term for advocates of independent states. Those who currently favored greater independence for states became known as "antifederalists."

Among the federalists were Alexander Hamilton, James Madison, and John Jay, who became the first Chief Justice of the U.S. Supreme Court. These three men wrote numerous papers, which were published in several New York newspapers as *The Federalist* essays. Today these essays are considered classic expressions of how freedom-loving people should be governed. Madison, for example, warned against factions, or special groups, that could easily gain and abuse power in independent states.

Others whose names are now well known in U.S. history opposed the constitution. Patrick Henry of Virginia, a champion of the revolution, was part of the opposition. He declared in a speech at the Virginia Ratification Conference that the confederation had "carried us through a long and dangerous war; it rendered us victorious in the bloody conflict with a powerful nation; it has secured us a territory greater than any European monarch possesses."

That government should not be abandoned, he argued, because "the ropes and chains" of a strong union would

> convert this country into a powerful and mighty empire. If you make the citizens of this country agree to become the subjects of one great consolidated empire of America, your government will not have sufficient energy to keep them together.[8]

Henry's arguments were strong, but after a three-week convention, Virginia's delegates approved the constitution 89 to 79, just a few days after the required ninth state, New Hampshire, had ratified it on June 21, 1788. Although the Constitution became the law of the land with New Hampshire's approval, ratification by Virginia and New York was particularly important toward gaining general acceptance of the Constitution. New York ratified it on July 26, 1788. In reality, to be effective, the new nation needed the support of all the states, and by 1790, each of the original thirteen states had voted for ratification.

More Fighting

Americans made great strides in the two decades after they won their independence and established a nation. But whatever the accomplishments, they were not necessarily made under peaceful conditions. Trade abroad, for example, often was subject to armed conflict and piracy.

In the years after James Madison became president in 1809, U.S. troops fought to gain territory claimed by Native Americans, and once again prepared to fight Great Britain in a conflict known as the War of 1812. That war ended in a famous battle at New Orleans led by Andrew Jackson, who became an American hero and eventually president of the United States.

The Treaty of Ghent officially brought hostilities to an end in 1815, and Americans turned their attention to forging a country that would be equal among the world's powers. War's end also prompted more expansion west, requiring the federal government to deal with leaders of other nations and indigenous people (Native Americans) who claimed vast amounts of territory. This expansion and pursuit of land led to more battles and many more lost lives.

When the United States expanded its territory,
conflicts arose between the U.S. military and
Native Americans, who resented being forced off
their traditional hunting grounds and homelands.

2

FIGHTING FOR TERRITORY

"The war has renewed and reinstated the national feelings and character which the Revolution had given," noted Secretary of the Treasury Albert Gallatin after the end of the second war with Great Britain. "The people now feel and act more as a nation."[1]

The war's end prompted not only a sense of nationalism in the United States, but also a period of remarkable growth. From 1815 to about 1850, the United States began to define itself and to fulfill what was called the nation's "manifest destiny." This term was coined in 1845 by New York newspaper editor John L. O'Sullivan when he wrote that it was "the fulfillment of our manifest destiny to overspread the continent allotted by Providence for the free development of our yearly expanding millions."[2] In other words, according to many in the country, the new peoples of the North American continent had a divine right to occupy the land and claim the resources they discovered from the Atlantic to the Pacific Oceans.

There was another side to this equation, however. Indigenous tribes and other people of color were often destroyed—killed, jailed, or enslaved—as pioneering Americans attempted to carry out their "manifest destiny." Many battles for territory created tremendous upheaval and loss of liberty or life for thousands in the years that followed the War of 1812.

SETTING THE STAGE FOR EXPANSION

While a peace of sorts prevailed, politics and economics played important roles in the nation's rapid expansion toward the Mississippi River and beyond. The U.S. Constitution made no provision for political parties, but two distinct and opposing groups emerged in the late 1790s: the Federalists, led by Hamilton, and the Democratic-Republicans (antifederalists), under the leadership of Jefferson and Madison. These groups paved the way for formal political parties that were organized years later, such as the Democratic and Republican parties today.

The Federalists favored a centralized government. Perhaps of greatest importance to the developing economy, they created a national bank to help guarantee credit and loans to businesses that were ready to grow. This atmosphere fueled an expansion of new industry, especially in New England, bringing added revenue to the federal government. Within a few years, Hamilton, then secretary of the treasury, was able to reduce the Revolutionary War debt.

Whatever the accomplishments, many Americans did not like giving the federal government power at the expense of the states. The nation's first president, George Washington, had taken great pains to avoid a "royal," or kingly, presidency, but antifederalists still considered his government an untrustworthy replacement for the despised British rule.

Working-class Scottish and German immigrants in the industrial north also distrusted a government that seemed to cater to business interests. In the election of 1800, they combined with the traditional antifederalists to choose Thomas Jefferson as president.

Jefferson encouraged democratic and populist ideals and practices in his government. As the chief architect of the Declaration of Independence, he believed government should protect individual rights (or at least the rights of free males). Because of his influence, many states, for example, eased voting requirements and reduced penalties for debtors.

One of Jefferson's outstanding decisions, however, had little to do with the rights of individuals. In 1803 he began negotiations with Napoleon Bonaparte, emperor of France, who had won from Spain an 800,000-square-mile tract of land in North America known as the Louisiana Territory. Americans feared that Napoleon intended to expand his empire by establishing settlements up and down the Mississippi River, the eastern boundary of the territory.

In fact, Napoleon planned to grow food in the fertile Mississippi valleys and ship it out of the port of New Orleans to the intended hub of his empire, the island of Hispaniola (Haiti). But in 1801 he had to send French troops to the island to put down a rebellion by the slave leader Toussaint L'Ouverture, who had seized control. Thousands of French soldiers died in the fighting or from yellow fever.

About the same time, a war with France's old enemy England was looming. Napoleon knew that he could not maintain control of the Louisiana Territory without a substantial investment of people and resources, so he made a very practical decision. He offered the land to Jefferson's representatives, one of whom was James Monroe.

Monroe and his colleagues were stunned when Napoleon offered to sell the Louisiana Territory for $15 million. But there was a problem: the Constitution had made no provision for the federal government to buy land.

At first Jefferson wanted to try to amend the Constitution, but his advisers warned against delay. Napoleon might change his mind. So Jefferson went ahead with the purchase, saying that the "good sense of our country" would correct the "ill effects" of a loosely constructed U.S. Constitution.

The Louisiana Territory doubled the size of the nation and encouraged the increasing population of European immigrants along the eastern seaboard to migrate westward. Many traveled the Ohio River singing a popular tune of the time, "Hi-o, away we go, floating down the river on the O-hi-o."

THE FRONTIER MIGRATION

After the War of 1812, work on the Erie Canal began. It was completed in 1825, connecting New York City to the Great Lakes of the Northwest Territory, and settlers poured into the plains around the lakes. Chicago, which began as a small fur trading settlement on the southwestern edge of Lake Michigan, became the commercial and trade center for vast expanses of family-owned farms.

Driven by the desire to improve their economic situation, pioneers also set out to occupy regions farther west. The first to explore the new territories were fur trappers and traders. These hardy men learned the ways of the wilderness and of the native tribes, which they relied on for trade. Many of them married Indian women and adopted the Native American way of life.

Those who followed the trappers, however, seldom respected Native American ways. Cattlemen, for example, looked for bigger and safer grasslands to raise their livestock. This inevitably led to conflicts with Native Americans over hunting grounds.

Farm families also headed for the Far West to claim parcels that the government offered free or for only $200 in the Oregon and California Territories. From 1841 to 1866, an estimated 350,000 men, women, and children traveled west in trains of covered wagons, known as prairie schooners because they were built for both overland travel and river crossings.[3]

But there was seldom smooth sailing. Wagons followed trails along muddy paths and rough roads, through swamps, across streams, and through treacherous mountain passes. On a journey of six to nine months, many people and animals died from accidents such as drownings or falls from wagons and from poisonous water and diseases. One sixteen-year-old on the trail was near death from what was called mountain fever and begged her mother to bury her in "a Grave six feet deep for she did nat [sic] want the wolves to dig her up and eat her."[4]

Miners, some accompanied by their families, were also part of the great migrations west. When "gold fever" was high in the 1850s, fourteen-year-old Rebecca Woodson and her family joined a wagon train heading for the gold fields. The adults, Rebecca wrote, expected "to amass very large fortunes" but the young ones like herself anticipated having "a whole lot of fun and pleasure."[5]

Very few of these gold panners found their fortunes in the streams of northern California, Colorado, or anywhere else in the West. The real legacy of the mining movement was in the towns and cities that were established and quickly grew.

In almost all regions where white settlers pushed west, they took over territory belonging to Native American tribes. In some cases, tribal chiefs were convinced they and their people would benefit from land deals, but they often lost their hunting grounds and homelands because of deceptive treaties or because U.S. soldiers forced them out.

CONFLICTS WITH NATIVE AMERICANS

Battles with Native Americans over land rights had been going on since the days when the first settlers arrived on the continent. During and after the War of 1812 those fights continued.

One military operation in 1816 was against Fort Negro on the Apalachicola River in Florida. The fort was in Spanish territory, and gaining land from Spain was the main purpose of the operation. But another goal was to kill the Seminoles who had taken refuge there. The Seminoles had been raiding pioneer settlements, and they also protected numerous escaped slaves, some of whom had intermarried with Seminoles and become leaders.

U.S. gunboats sailed up the Apalachicola and officers demanded that those in the fort surrender. When they refused, the gunboats prepared to fire. On July 27, 1816, the fort was blown up. One of the officers reporting on the explosion noted that the sight was

> horrible beyond description . . . The war yells of the Indians, the cries and lamentations of the wounded, compel'd the soldier to pause in the midst of victory, and to drop a tear for the sufferings of his fellow beings, and to acknowledge that the great ruler of the Universe must have used us as an instrument in chastising the blood thirsty murderous wretches that defended the Fort.[6]

While most army officers of the time were certain they were justified in ridding the country of "murderous wretches" who harbored escaped slaves, Seminole chiefs had a different view. One chief complained mightily that settlers caused conflicts, and that his tribe protected "no Negroes." Rather, the chief asserted, "When the Englishmen were at war with America, some [Negroes] took shelter among them; and it is for you white people to settle those things among yourselves, and not trouble us with what we know nothing about."[7]

Native Americans were also subjected to much pressure from speculators and government officials who tried to convince tribal leaders to sell their land and consolidate in one place. The Buffalo Creek Reservation of the Seneca tribe might have been sold quickly except for the strong objections of their leader, Red Jacket. He was incensed that President James Monroe (elected in 1816) would suggest that it was in the Seneca interest to sell their land. Addressing a meeting of U.S. officials and the Seneca, Red Jacket declared, "The President must have been disordered in mind, or he would not offer to lead us off by the arms."[8]

Yet some northern tribal chiefs did not agree. During the 1820s they signed agreements to sell their land for 53¢ an acre, forcing their people to move elsewhere.

INDIAN REMOVALS

In 1828 Andrew Jackson was elected president, and he made no secret of his belief that Indians should be sent as far west of the Mississippi River as possible. This policy was bolstered with passage of the Indian Removal Act of 1830. Subsequently, thousands of Cherokee, Chickasaw, Choctaw, Creek, and Seminole in the Southeast were forced to move to what was later named the Oklahoma Territory.

Some tribes fought back but were defeated. The Cherokee tried to win their battle in court, but this attempt also failed. Their removal to the western territory was along a route they called the "trail of tears" because fifteen hundred died of disease and starvation on the way.

Indian removals continued through the 1840s and 1850s. In 1851 the Eastern Dakotas gave up all of their lands and were relocated to a reservation in west-central Minnesota. Throughout the next dozen or more years, Dakotas faced numerous obstacles, including failed crops and a refusal by the U.S. government to provide food for their starving people. The federal government's broken promises and threats to evict the Dakota from their reservation led to war and attacks on settlers in 1862.

Dakota warriors were soon defeated by the U.S. Army. About six thousand Dakotas fled from the state, and another two thousand were captured and imprisoned. More than three hundred Dakota men were condemned to death by a military court, but President Abraham Lincoln, "in a compromise decision," commuted the sentences for all but thirty-eight men, who were "hanged before a crowd of 3,000 in Mankato, Minnesota. It remains the largest mass execution in U.S. history."[9]

During the winter of 1863, the remaining prisoners were sent by railroad boxcar and steamboat to the Crow Creek Reservation on the Missouri River in Dakota Territory. Here, many died from starvation and exposure. In the meantime, "the free Dakota were left scattered across the plains, as their lands were confiscated by the federal government and sold to benefit the white victims of the conflict. To this day, the Dakota have received little or no compensation for their lands" in Minnesota.[10]

The federal government also imposed numerous changes in tribal customs and beliefs. But many observances continued in secret. "I remember my mother said when she was little, they would have a PowWow or 'Wacipi' and cover up all the windows with blankets, so no light could go out," Darlene Renville Pipeboy recalled. And Alvina Alberts noted: "We were oppressed people. But we can say that we have survived."[11]

A TEXAS REVOLT

As with Native American lands, the U.S. government used armed force to win territory from Mexico. About thirty thousand U.S. settlers lived in Coahuila–Texas, a huge Mexican state that later became known as the Texas Territory. Most settlers were from southern states and had become Mexican citizens.

Texas settlers, however, disliked Mexican rule, particularly laws against slavery. They began a revolt, which led to a now-famous siege at the Alamo, an abandoned Catholic mission. In February 1836 about 180 Texans fortified themselves in the mission to hold off at least two thousand Mexican troops led by General Santa Anna. After days of siege, the Mexican army attacked. In a bloody battle that ended on March 6, 1836, all inside the Alamo were killed. But the deaths stirred even more determination for independence, symbolized by the rallying cry, "Remember the Alamo."

A Texas army led by Sam Houston, who had fought in the War of 1812 and had been a Tennessee governor, captured Santa Anna in April 1836. The general was forced to sign a treaty granting independence to Texas.

Settlers continued to arrive in the Texas Territory, among them prosperous plantation families such as that of Samuel Augustus Maverick. Maverick had fought in the Texas revolt and was thirty-three years old when he married eighteen-year-old Mary Adams from Tuscaloosa County, Alabama, in August 1836. In December of the following year, they moved with their five-month-old child to San Antonio, Texas, where they settled on a large homestead.

During her first years there, Mary Maverick, like others of her time, recorded a number of encounters with various tribal groups. She described a "day of horrors" in 1840, when "sixty-five Comanches came into town to make a treaty of peace," Maverick wrote. "They brought with them, and reluctantly gave up, Matilda Lockhart, whom they had captured with her younger sister in December 1838, after killing two other children of her family."[12]

The chiefs and several military officers met in the council room of the courthouse, intending to make a peace agreement, but the Comanches wanted "paint, powder, flannel, blankets and such other articles" in exchange for captives they still held. Officers refused to pay the ransom because the

Comanches had previously made such deals but had killed their captives and kept the bounty. When the officers made a counteroffer to hold four chiefs until the Texans were released, the courthouse became a battleground. As Maverick reported, the Comanches

> raised a terrific war-whoop, drew their arrows, and commenced firing with deadly effect, at the same time making efforts to break out of the council hall. The order "fire" was given . . . and the soldiers fired into the midst of the crowd, the first volley killing several Indians and two of our own people. All soon rushed out into the public square, the civilians to procure arms, the Indians to flee, and the soldiers in pursuit . . . . Not one of the sixty-five Indians escaped—thirty-three were killed and thirty-two were taken prisoners. Six Americans and one Mexican were killed and ten Americans wounded.[13]

In 1842 the Mavericks moved to eastern Texas because of rumors that Mexico was preparing to attack San Antonio. They returned to San Antonio in 1847, two years after Texas was annexed to the United States. But a dispute with Mexico over where to locate the border of Texas led to a fight between the two nations that lasted from 1846 to 1848.

Although many easterners thought that the Mexican War was just an excuse to grab more territory for the United States, the war effort received enthusiastic support from westerners. The volunteer army increased from six thousand to over 115,000. While some troops were invading the southern portions of Mexico to seal victory over a weak government there, other forces cut off the northern half of that country— now the states of New Mexico and California.

The war took a heavy toll on U.S. soldiers, as wounds and diseases caused a 35 percent casualty rate, the worst such statistic of any American war. The 1848 Treaty of Guadalupe Hidalgo ended the fighting, and one of its main provisions authorized the United States to take over the captured area in exchange for $15 million. Five years later, the United States paid Mexico another $10 million in a deal known as the Gadsden Purchase for a strip of land that created the final southern boundaries of New Mexico and Arizona.

The development of the railroad in the United States began
about 1827. The rail system soon played a major role in the
economic growth of the nation. The steam locomotive shown
here was in service in 1836.

3

BETWEEN WARS

"It is only in the light of history that the effects of [Texas] annexation can be fully comprehended, coupled as it is with the history of the Mexican war, and the discovery of gold in California. It is only in the light of history that we shall be able to read the now silent workings of a new and peculiar phase of civilization," Teresa Griffin Vielé, an army wife, wrote in the 1850s.[1]

In her account about the Texas frontier, Vielé's words seem prophetic. But she had no idea what the new "phase of civilization" would bring.

Before and after the Mexican War and annexation of Texas as a slave state, the issue of slavery increasingly polarized Northern and Southern states. Violent conflicts erupted over the admission of western states: the North wanted slavery abolished in new states, and the South wanted states to maintain it.

At the same time, a strife-ridden labor movement was attempting to improve working conditions for thousands. Against tremendous opposition, women were struggling for civil rights, and states were trying to make educational reforms, including setting up public school systems. In short, the nation suffered growing pains during the 1850s. But by the 1860s its growth and very life were threatened.

PAVING THE WAY FOR GROWTH

While the well-known *New York Tribune* editor Horace Greeley in 1850 urged young men to "go West . . . and grow up with the country," other writers and orators advised people to join the work force in the many new industries that had developed, especially in the East. The New England states enjoyed an economic boom during this time of relative peace.

In the United States, especially in the North, the situation was ripe for the type of changes that remarkable advances in science and technology made possible. The development of railroad systems was a prime example. It started in 1827, when merchants in Maryland's capital chartered the Baltimore & Ohio Railroad to increase trade with the western territories. The South Carolina Railroad began service soon afterward with the first steam locomotive, which was called Best Friend of Charleston. Within ten years the rail lines became an accepted and reliable system for the transport of people, food, and manufactured goods throughout most of the nation.

The rails were also used to transport one other important commodity: newspapers. Advances in printing technology had made production faster and less expensive than ever before, and U.S. newspapers and other publications became affordable for most people.

The first developments in telecommunications were also taking place. Joseph Henry, a physicist who developed electromagnetic principles during the 1820s and 1830s, made it possible for Samuel F. B. Morse to invent the telegraph and to create a language of dots and dashes (the Morse Code) to send and receive messages over great distances. Telegraph systems were deployed throughout the rail lines of the United States, and they were eventually expanded to include most population centers.

Along with new technology, businesses had access to great supplies of natural resources and manufacturing expertise. Ready credit sources and good markets created a perfect environment for the economy to grow. Business leaders were also ready to adopt the factory system that was already in place in European countries.

Samuel Slater was one of the first to apply this method of manufacturing when he copied the design of successful textile mills that were operating in his native Great Britain. He brought these ideas to Rhode Island, where he opened a cotton mill in 1792. Other investors such as Francis Cabot Lowell and his Boston Associates saw the advantages of bringing the workers into factories and out of their homes, where the work had always been done. This move led to cost savings, because the means of production could be centralized.

Lowell first set up a textile factory in Waltham, Massachusetts. Then in 1822 he and his associates built on another site that eventually became a factory town called Lowell. Similar towns grew up and prospered, and other factories for making tin, iron, clocks, paper, and glass seemed to spring up like weeds all over New England.

Between the 1820s and the 1850s, when the Industrial Revolution took hold in America, the means of production changed from the work of individual craftsmen in rural settings to the industrial output of armies of workers in cities. Thousands of immigrants also came to cities, increasing the urban population, which totaled well over two million by 1860. With the increased population came overcrowded and unsafe housing, hazardous work conditions, and exploitation of workers.

Most laborers of the 1800s worked from sunup to sundown for low pay. Men with picks and shovels labored daily on railroads and canals for fifteen to sixteen hours, earning as little as 15¢ a day.

In the New England textile mills, employees were predominantly young women and girls. Girls were enticed with propaganda about the benefits of living and working in "spindle cities," as textile mill towns were called. Mill owners paid poets to write songs describing the advantages of mill life.

One verse claimed girls at the loom were healthy and happy, "merry and glad and free!"[2] Another asserted that girls "cheerfully talketh away" while watching the spindle.[3] But in reality, there was little freedom and cheer. For $1 to $2 per week plus board, the girls were compelled to work fourteen to sixteen hours a day. Their living quarters were cramped, sometimes with six girls to a room and two to a bed.[4] Factories were poorly ventilated and hazardous to health and safety.

Trade unions had been organized since the late 1700s, and by the 1830s more and more workers were calling for a ten-hour work day, enforcing their demands with strikes. But employers simply hired "scabs"—workers willing to take the jobs of strikers. The struggle went on well into the next century.

EARLY REFORM MOVEMENTS

As the labor movement fought for changes for the benefit of workers, other types of reform efforts also marked the first half of the nineteenth century. For example, reformers crusaded against the filthy and inhumane conditions of prisons and dungeons where the destitute, the insane, and hardened criminals were jailed together. Dorothea Dix, a young Boston teacher, became famous for investigating the treatment of the insane in Massachusetts and crusading to establish mental hospitals supported by the state. In 1843 she reported to the state legislature that insane persons were kept "in cages, closets, cellars, stalls, pens! Chained, naked, beaten with rods, and lashed into obedience."[5] Dix's efforts continued throughout her life and gradually achieved changes in mental institutions in her state and in others across the nation.

Educational reforms, especially efforts to achieve equality in education, began also. By the 1840s, women had gained access to basic schooling, which was denied them during the Revolutionary period. Girls at that time were considered fit only for homemaking and child care. But with the industrial revolution, girls and women found jobs outside the home, in factories. They also were needed to teach the increasing population in the cities.

During the first half of the 1800s there was still widespread prejudice against educating females, but some courageous and persistent women opened schools for girls. In 1821 Emma Willard, for example, founded the Troy Female Seminary in Troy, New York. The school introduced girls to algebra, geometry, geography, and domestic science. Willard also taught what was then a taboo subject for women, physiology. According to one historian's report,

> Mothers visiting a class at the Seminary in the early thirties were so shocked at the sight of a pupil drawing a heart, arteries and veins on a blackboard to explain the circulation of the blood, that they left the room in shame and dismay. To preserve the modesty of the girls . . . heavy paper was pasted over the pages in their textbooks which depicted the human body.[6]

Campaigns for public schools made gains during the 1830s and 1840s, and tax-supported elementary schools were set up in most states. But these schools were predominantly white. There were no schools for blacks in the South, and in the North, there were usually separate schools for students of color.

A few daring individuals opened private schools that admitted blacks. In 1833 Prudence Crandall enrolled black girls in her Canterbury, Connecticut, school, which she set up in her own home. She faced opposition from her church and threats of violence from townspeople. One of her students wrote that merchants in Canterbury "are *savage*—they will not sell Miss Crandall an article from their shops." Townspeople also raised loud protests, blowing horns and firing pistols when the girls left school for the day. Still, "in the midst of all this Miss Crandall is unmoved," the student wrote.[7] Eventually, though, Crandall was forced to close her school after a mob with clubs and iron bars attacked the house, endangering the lives of her students.

In Canaan, New Hampshire, similar attacks in 1835 drove three black males away from a school—or more accurately, a white mob took the school away from them. The black students, who had been invited to enroll and had traveled four hundred miles to get to the school, "met a most cordial reception . . . from two score white students," Alexander Crummell, a black student, reported. But within two months farmers "from a wide region around . . . gathered together . . . seized the building, and with ninety yoke of oxen carried it off into a swamp about a half mile from its site. They were two days in accomplishing this miserable work," Crummell wrote.[8]

Oberlin College in Ohio was the first college to open its doors to students regardless of gender or color. Among its famous graduates was Lucy Stone. While at Oberlin, Lucy Stone had prepared herself to speak out for women's rights, including the right to vote. She was also adamantly opposed to slavery. A year after her graduation in 1847 she became a lecturer for the Anti-Slavery Society. She believed that the abolition of slavery and women's rights were entwined. Her views were shared by such women as Lucretia Mott, Elizabeth Cady Stanton, and sisters Sarah and Angelina Grimké. All of these women became well known as bold advocates for equal rights, regardless of gender and color.

However, many abolitionists were opposed to combining slavery and women's rights issues. They believed the two should be separated, tackling slavery first because it was a foremost moral and social evil.

Abolitionists focused on the physical cruelties of slavery—the terrible beatings and mutilations that some suffered, the breakup of families, and the dehumanization of people in chains. Though some slaves were more kindly treated, the concept that one person could own another was never acceptable to abolitionists. And they opposed the tough 1850 Fugitive Slave Act that provided for a hefty fine and six months in prison for helping slaves escape.

Many abolitionists, including Quakers, helped slaves escape through the Underground Railroad System, secret routes from southern to northern states or to Canada. The Canadian government had made it clear that Canada did "not know men by their color." They invited African Americans to "come to us [and] you will be entitled to all the privileges" of other Canadians.[9] The courageous Harriet Tubman, a former slave, led at least three hundred other escapees along the Underground Railroad to freedom.

Abolitionists organized numerous antislavery lectures and conferences to build political opposition to slavery. Frederick Douglass, a fugitive slave, became a famous orator for the cause and often was threatened and attacked by proslavery mobs.

Abolitionists also sent hundreds of antislavery appeals to the U.S. Congress, a practice that began in the late 1700s and increased during the 1800s. One congressman, former president John Quincy Adams of Massachusetts, introduced more than three hundred such petitions in 1838 and opposed annexing Texas as a slave state.

Some abolitionists were determined to end slavery by any means necessary, including violence. A free black man, David

Walker, and Henry Garnet, an escaped slave, were two abolitionists who urged slaves to revolt, to be willing to die for their liberty and to kill their oppressors if necessary. Nat Turner's rebellion in 1831 resulted in the death of more than fifty whites and Turner himself.

Whites who advocated radical action included William Lloyd Garrison, founder of a newspaper called the *Liberator*. In his first issue, published January 1, 1831, Garrison announced, "I shall strenuously contend for the immediate enfranchisement of our slave population . . . . On this subject I do not wish to think, or speak, or write with moderation . . . . I am in earnest—I will not equivocate—I will not excuse—I will not retreat a single inch and I WILL BE HEARD."[10]

THE GREAT DIVISION

In spite of the widespread debate and action to free slaves, most white Northerners were not especially interested in their fate. For one thing, there were few slaves in the North. Northern states had outlawed slavery before abolitionist groups became active in the 1800s. It was simply not economical to keep slaves for work on northern farms that were nearly idle in the winter months.

Although some Southerners embraced the antislavery cause, most people in the South feared abolitionists. The South did not experience the same economic growth as the North, although its importance to the country was growing because of the cotton boom. This cash crop was in high demand as a source of cloth and other products in New England and in the West. More important, Europeans prized cotton, and many farmers were able to export their products abroad in exchange for gold and stable foreign currency. The Southern economy was built on the labor of slaves who were as much the property of the "gentlemen farmers" as were the cows, plows, or cotton rows of the plantations, and the economy rewarded white landowners well.

The culture that developed in the South also created institutions and laws that supported slavery. Southerners justified bondage in numerous ways. Often whites claimed that they were "naturally superior" to the "savages" and needed to "civilize" them. Some declared that the Bible required blacks to be subservient to their white masters. These and other ideas of white supremacy were carefully taught to slave and free alike.

The North and South were not only divided by economics and culture, they were also separated by the Mason-Dixon line. This geographic line originally marked the border between Pennsylvania and its southern neighbor, Maryland. It was surveyed between 1763 and 1767 by two Englishmen, Charles Mason and Jeremiah Dixon, who were asked to settle a boundary dispute between the states.

In 1820, when there were heated arguments over slavery in the territories of the Louisiana Purchase, Congress made a decision known as the Missouri Compromise. It allowed slavery in the states south of the Mason-Dixon Line. Congress declared the line extended from the original survey out to the Rocky Mountains along the 36 degree 30 minute parallel. Above that line slavery was to remain illegal.

While the Missouri Compromise helped ease the differences between the North and South for a few years, the compromise ended with the Kansas-Nebraska Act of 1854. The act opened up the slavery question to popular choice in the western territories.

When Abraham Lincoln was elected president in 1860, he did not advocate outlawing slavery in the South. Nevertheless, Southerners were convinced that Lincoln's administration would end the practice. This mistrust and the real differences in economies and cultures between the two sections of the country motivated seven states, led by South Carolina, to secede from the Union before Lincoln was inaugurated. Four more states joined the Confederate rebellion by the spring of 1861, and the Civil War had begun. Four years and over 600,000 lives later, the South was vanquished.

As the nation recovered after the Civil War, iron and steel production became huge industries. Large cities sprang up, and a network of railroads moved manufactured goods across the nation.

4

REBUILDING

"To-day a nation sits down beneath the shadow of mournful grief. Oh, what a terrible lesson does this even read to us!" wrote black poet Frances Ellen Watkins Harper a few days after President Abraham Lincoln was assassinated on April 15, 1865.[1]

Several decades later a former officer with the New York volunteers in the Union Army declared:

> the South came . . . to realise how great had been the loss, for its own pressing needs, in the death of the . . . President. Lincoln . . . would have given in full measure his thought and vitality to the service of the great communities that were now desolate and that were in urgent need of the guidance of the National Government . . . The discouraging and mortifying experiences of the reconstruction years would have been avoided or would at least have been very much minimised." [2]

Lincoln's death at the hand of Confederate sympathizer John Wilkes Booth came just six days after General Robert E. Lee surrendered the rebel army at Appomattox Courthouse, officially ending the most tragic episode in the nation's history. Some 2,250,000 white, black, and Indian men had fought under President Lincoln to preserve the union in the great Civil War. The Confederate States of America had fielded a much smaller force of about 750,000 under their president, Jefferson Davis. Though Confederates fought with a passion that stemmed from the defense of their agrarian way of life, they lacked resources. Lincoln knew that it was only a matter of time until the Confederacy was brought down, and he hoped to reconcile the differences between the combatants.

To do this, Lincoln first proclaimed that secession was not legal under the Constitution, and therefore, it had not occurred. He devised a plan that would allow a new government to be formed in any of the rebellious states if 10 percent of the voters would sign a loyalty oath to the United States of America. In his second, now famous, inaugural speech delivered a month before his death, he asked the nation to harbor no malice and "strive on to finish the work we are in; to bind up the nation's wounds . . . to do all which may achieve and cherish a just and lasting peace among ourselves and with all nations."

Lincoln wanted to give the South every opportunity to rejoin the Union quickly and restore the country. It would have required a deft and skilled politician to drive this concept through Congress. Lincoln might have had a chance, but his successor, Andrew Johnson, had very little.

BEGINNINGS OF RECONSTRUCTION

In 1860 Andrew Johnson was a U.S. senator, a Democrat from Tennessee. He was a passionate defender of states' rights, as were many in the Democratic party at that time. As such, he had defended slavery as a right of the citizens of the Southern states, and he had stood with those who thought new territories in the 1840s and 1850s could legally decide to make slavery part of their codes. However, he did agree with Lincoln, a Republican, that secession was an illegal act.

As senator, Johnson fought hard to keep his state in the Union, but to no avail. He was the only Southern congressmen who refused to resign from his position in the federal government, and in the presidential campaign of 1864 he was rewarded for his loyalty. He was chosen to run as Lincoln's vice-president in order to broaden the appeal of the Republican party's ticket.

When he succeeded Lincoln, Johnson tried to remain true to his predecessor's plan for a gentle transition back to a unified country. Congress, dominated by punitive Republicans, had already halted Lincoln's attempt to set up new governments in several Southern states (Louisiana, Tennessee, and Arkansas). Republican senators and representatives refused to allow the new officials from those governments, mostly Democrats, to take their seats in Congress. Instead, they proposed a law, known as the Wade-Davis Reconstruction Bill, that would require 50 percent of voters to swear their loyalty to the U.S. government.

Lincoln had allowed the Wade-Davis bill to die in 1864 with a pocket veto—he did not sign it. Johnson, however, tried to accommodate some of the provisions in the measure. New states were required to ratify the Thirteenth Amendment, which officially freed the slaves, and to abolish slavery in their own constitutions. At the same time, Johnson declared a broad amnesty to anyone who would pledge loyalty to the United States in the future. This hastened the formation of new governments throughout the former Confederacy.

THE FREEDMEN'S BUREAU

During the time that new state governments were forming, the federal Bureau of Refugees, Freedmen, and Abandoned Lands of the War Department, commonly known as the Freedmen's Bureau, began operations in the South. Established just before the end of the war, the bureau had several goals: provide supplies and medical services for ex-slaves and refugees; help freed blacks gain employment and fair wages; manage lands that had been confiscated or abandoned in the South; and set up schools. This period was called Reconstruction.

Though there was poor management and some corruption within the bureau, it established more than forty hospitals and helped resettle thirty thousand displaced people within a four-year period. Its greatest achievement was in education, overseeing forty-three hundred schools. These included day schools for children and universities such as Howard and Fisk, which still operate today. Night classes for adults who had to work all day were also set up. Young and old were eager to learn and, in fact, thousands had tried to educate themselves even when schooling for blacks was illegal. One bureau official in North Carolina noted in 1866, "A child six years old, her mother, grandmother, and great-grandmother, the latter over 75 years of age . . . commenced their alphabet together and each one can read the Bible fluently."[3]

Teachers were predominantly women and came from across the United States to work in these schools, which were often log houses, some without floors or windows. The teachers faced numerous difficulties, especially when threatened by whites who hated the bureau and did not want blacks to be educated. Opponents threw bricks and other objects at schools, burned down school buildings, and ran some teachers out of town.

Southerners especially resented the bureau's authority to set up courts and settle civil or criminal disputes that involved former slaves. To Southerners, the bureau represented federal interference in state affairs, and officials were often attacked and beaten. For protection, one Tennessee agent said he kept "a double-barreled shot gun, heavily charged at one hand and a hatchet at the other." [4]

RADICAL REPUBLICANS

President Johnson was outspoken about his objections to the Freedmen's Bureau and vetoed a bill extending its life, which

Congress overrode. Even though Johnson had been adamant about preserving the Union during the war, he was still an ardent white supremacist and became increasingly hostile to members of Congress who advocated equality for black people. Johnson's position prompted many moderate Republicans to join so-called radical Republicans who were driven by a desire to see the former Confederacy punished.

The radicals pushed through laws that provided for military governments in states that had seceded. Radicals also developed Reconstruction plans based on the idea that former slaves be granted basic human rights within their states. In 1866 Congress passed the Fourteenth Amendment, which was key to these Reconstruction plans. It was probably the most important change to the Constitution since the Bill of Rights was adopted.

The amendment counteracted the "Black Codes" that the newly formed state governments had sanctioned. These codes simply modified old slave laws that had been on the books since before the war, and effectively denied social, economic, and political equality to newly freed blacks. The Fourteenth Amendment stated, "All persons born or naturalized in the United States and subject to the jurisdiction thereof, are citizens of the United States and of the states in which they reside." The amendment forbade any state from enacting laws that would deny any class of citizens their rights under the Constitution.

When it came to approving the amendment, Northern states hardly set an example for the South. Only two, Connecticut and New Hampshire, ratified the Fourteenth Amendment within one month. In some states, debates over approval were bitter. But by 1868, the amendment was ratified. Its enactment meant that the balance of political power was significantly shifted from the states to the federal government, which now had the final word about laws passed at the local level.

President Johnson tried to delay or circumvent the desires of the Republicans. He openly sided with the Southern

Democrats, who opposed continued military occupation. The Democrats also despised Southern "scalawags," Republicans, and northern "carpetbaggers," so called because many supposedly came South with all their belongings in a carpet bag. The conflict between the president and Congress became so heated that Johnson was impeached in 1868. In his Senate trial, he was acquitted by only two votes, but the action left him powerless. Ulysses S. Grant was elected president soon afterward.

Congress went on with its plan to empower the former slaves. In 1869 it passed the Fifteenth Amendment, which proclaimed that the right to vote "shall not be denied . . . on account of race, color, or previous condition of servitude," and despite much opposition, was ratified in 1870. Although a few blacks had previously won political office, the number of elected black officials increased. Between 1868 and 1877, nearly two thousand black men were elected, including the first blacks to sit in the U.S Congress, Senator Hiram Revels of Mississippi, seated February 23, 1870, and Representative Joseph H. Rainey of South Carolina, seated December 12, 1870.

But this progress did not come peacefully. Southern whites generally opposed racial equality, and they especially hated that their northern-supported state governments were being dominated by Republicans, and in some cases by former slaves. Terrorism and outbreaks of violence became commonplace.

THE RISE OF THE KKK

One of the first terrorist groups in the United States, the Ku Klux Klan (KKK), began in Pulaski, Tennessee. At first the KKK was like a social club, a secret society made up of Confederate veterans. To amuse themselves, they often dressed in sheets to conceal their identity and played practical jokes on new recruits. Members, however, soon became formally organized under former Confederate General Nathan B. Forrest and as a group began to harass blacks in the South.

Because black votes helped put Republicans into office in Southern states, the Klan retaliated by brutally attacking blacks or anyone who sympathized with Republicans in power. "During the late 1860s, the Klan spread its reign of terror throughout Southern and border states," wrote historian Kathleen M. Blee. "Gangs of Klansmen threatened, flogged, and murdered countless black and white women and men . . . . Schoolteachers, revenue collectors, election officials, and Republican officeholders—those most involved with dismantling parts of the racial state—as well as all black persons, were the most common targets of Klan terror."[5]

The KKK was supported by many Democrats in the South, either through actual participation in the lynchings of blacks and white sympathizers, or by simply looking the other way when the Klansmen went on a rampage. In most states authorities were reluctant to suppress the violence with their mostly black militias because they feared a race war. Congress finally took action in 1871 and authorized President Ulysses S. Grant to send in federal soldiers to hold suspected terrorists in jail without trial. The Klan collapsed soon afterward.

The Klan did not disappear, however. Over the next few decades, the organization would revive for a time, die out, and then revive again, with leaders loudly proclaiming their belief in white—meaning white Anglo-Saxon Protestant (WASP)—supremacy. The KKK attacked not only African Americans but also Jews, Catholics, immigrants, and trade union members. Just before World War I, a Klan revival began in the state of Indiana and spawned factions throughout the Midwest, South, and West. The organization was romanticized in stories and films, such as D. W. Griffith's movie *The Birth of a Nation* (1915), which falsely portrays noble Klansmen defending Southern honor during Reconstruction. White supremacists still show and distribute this film.

While the Klan made a temporary resurgence throughout the 1920s, its membership has declined over the years. Today many Klan members are part of militant militias and other hate groups. The present existence of the KKK is a legacy of the institution of slavery and the failure of Reconstruction.

THE END OF RECONSTRUCTION

Most states of the former Confederacy had re-established legislatures dominated by white supremacists. New segregation ordinances called Jim Crow laws were passed. The name Jim Crow came from a minstrel tune that denigrated blacks.[6] These laws excluded blacks from white schools, churches, transportation facilities, and eating places. And literacy tests were imposed as a qualification for voting.

A large number of blacks found themselves back on the land of former slave owners, as sharecroppers, living in poverty and debt. A little more than a decade after the Civil War, equality for black people had been stifled, and by 1877 Reconstruction in the South was officially over. The nation turned its attention elsewhere.

TRANSITIONS

From the late 1870s through the beginning of the next century, people were on the move, involved in changes taking place nationwide. Manufacturing centers sprouted or expanded everywhere, creating cities where small towns had been. Growth created great bounty for a relatively small number of business tycoons, often called "robber barons" because of the ruthless manner by which they accumulated wealth at the expense of the majority, who lived and worked in miserable poverty conditions. It was a period sometimes called the Gilded Age, after the title of a novel by Mark Twain and Charles Dudley Warner that showed life's glossy surface covering blemishes underneath.

During the 1870s and 1880s in the Southwest, the "cattle kingdom" developed as Texas cowboys drove longhorns north to rail lines to be shipped to Chicago slaughterhouses.

Meat packing created huge fortunes for such men as Phillip Armour and Gustavus Swift.

In Pennsylvania, West Virginia, and Ohio, oil production was under way. By 1879 John D. Rockefeller had gained control of nearly all of the oil refining industry in the United States, which he dominated until 1892 when his huge trust was broken by the federal government.

Iron and steel production became huge industries and brought fortunes and luxurious lifestyles to such tycoons as Andrew Carnegie and J. Pierpont Morgan. But those who worked in the mills during the 1880s, including many children, received little in financial rewards and often worked under dangerous and unhealthy conditions. James L. Davis, who went on to become U.S. secretary of labor, began work in the Pittsburgh mills at twelve years old. In his later years he described how he melted pig iron in a furnace with intense heat:

> Vigorously I stoked that fire for thirty minutes with dampers open and the draft roaring while that pig-iron melted down like ice cream under an electric fan . . . . There were five bakings every day and this meant the shoveling in of nearly two tons of coal. In summer I was stripped to the waist and panting while the sweat poured down . . . . My palms and fingers, scorched by the heat, became hardened like goat hoofs, while my skin took on a coat of tan that it will wear forever.[7]

Iron and steel were basic materials for manufacturing such goods as mechanical harvesters, threshers, and binders, thereby helping agriculture to flourish. Printing presses were manufactured, leading to expanded communication. Increased sewing machine production brought about growth in such industries as shoe manufacturing and apparel.

In the South, tobacco and sugarcane production became important industries. Lumber mills sprang up, and shipbuilding, canneries, and distilleries flourished as well. Cotton was still the most important crop in the South, however, and cotton textile mills expanded from 161 in 1880 to four hundred in 1900. Eventually the South's textile production topped that of New England mills.[8]

Transportation systems that linked industrial centers, territories, and new states were vital to the nation's economic growth. Traffic increased on rivers, canals, and numerous new roadways. Even before the Civil War, government—both state and federal—had encouraged railroad growth with grants of land and money. Increased government aid after the Civil War resulted in tens of thousands of miles of new rail lines. From the late 1860s through the 1880s, numerous rail networks were completed, including the Southern Pacific; the Atchison, Topeka & Santa Fe; and the Missouri, Kansas, & Texas Railroads.

The most spectacular railroad accomplishments were the transcontinentals. The Union Pacific built a line from Nebraska to Promontory, Utah, and in 1869 met the Central Pacific line that began in San Francisco. For the first time east and west were linked by rail.

Laborers for the railroad, called rail gangs, included thousands of immigrants who swelled the nation's population after the war. Among them were Irish and German immigrants, who worked on eastern lines. Eleven thousand Chinese labored for a dollar a day on the Central Pacific and handled unstable explosives that frequently killed them, giving rise to the saying that there was not "a Chinaman's chance" to succeed.[9]

Railroad builders also faced numerous other life-threatening dangers as they constructed trestles over deep ravines and rivers and cut through rocks on steep mountain passes. Weather conditions, from blinding snowstorms to intense heat, were hazardous. And Native American tribes, angered by the encroachment on their lands, often attacked not only railroaders but also others migrating west, causing numerous Indian wars.

Hundreds of Native Americans and army troops were killed on battlefields that are now famous, such as Little Bighorn in Montana and Wounded Knee in South Dakota. When troops battled the Nez Perce and chased them for thirteen hundred miles across the Northwest, Chief Joseph, who always wanted to avoid war, was finally forced to surrender, saying

> I am tired of fighting . . . . It is cold and we have no blankets. The little children are freezing to death. My people, some of them, have run away to the hills and have no blankets, no food . . . . my heart is sick and sad. From where the sun now stands I will fight no more, forever.[10]

STILL ANOTHER WAR

While Native Americans were overpowered and numerous other people of color, immigrants, and laborers were exploited, the United States was on its way to becoming an industrial giant. But that did not seem enough. Before the end of the century, some Americans began talking about the nation's imperial destiny, following the example of European countries and creating a global empire. Business leaders and some government officials sought to increase trade and acquire more land that would produce goods ranging from tobacco and sugar to minerals and oil. And many clerics and missionaries wanted to save the world with their brand of Christianity.

Powerful forces seemed to propel the nation toward still another war. When newspapers began to sensationalize Spanish brutalities against the people of Cuba, a Spanish colony, calls for war were heard from many U.S. quarters. Then the U.S. battleship *Maine* sailed to the Havana harbor in Cuba and was mysteriously blown up in February 1898, killing 260. Within a few months, President William McKinley, who had tried to avert armed conflict, announced a declaration of war against Spain.

The Spanish-American War of 1898, dubbed the "splendid little war," lasted only a few months but resulted in more than 5,400 American deaths, most from diseases such as malaria and yellow fever. After a decisive victory, the United States acquired Cuba and Puerto Rico as possessions and gained control of Wake Island, Guam, and the Philippines.

In the years before World War I, labor unions formed. In late 1909 women shirtwaist workers in New York and Philadelphia struck for better working conditions and pay.

5

REBELS AND REFORMERS

After the Spanish-American War, Filipino rebels clearly demonstrated that they had no desire to be under U.S. rule. For three years they engaged in guerrilla warfare. During that time, many in the United States expressed their opposition to U.S. fighting in the Philippines. In 1900 leaders of groups working for Philippine independence issued an "Address to the Colored People of the United States," declaring that

> If ever there was a war of races in this world, the war now going on in the Philippine Islands is precisely that . . . . Every day in the Philippines is already training our young American soldiers to the habit of thinking that the white man . . . is the rightful ruler of all other men. This is seen, for instance, in the fact that these very soldiers, in writing home . . . describe the inhabitants of the Philippines, more and more constantly, as "niggers"; thus giving a new lease of life to a word which was previously dying out . . . .[1]

Indeed, many of the letters written by U.S. soldiers fighting in the Philippines belittled or showed racial hatred for their opponents. For example, a Utah private wrote that he was going on a "goo-goo hunt" for Filipinos and that

> no cruelty is too severe for these brainless monkeys, who can appreciate no sense of honor, kindness, or justice. . . . With an enemy like this to fight, it is not surprising that the boys should soon adopt 'no quarter' as a motto, and fill the blacks full of lead before finding out whether or not they are friends or enemies.[2]

In the opinion of other U.S. soldiers, however, Filipinos were "fighting for a good cause," as Ellis G. Davis of Kansas wrote, "and the Americans should be the last of all nations to transgress upon such rights. Their independence is dearer to them than life, as ours was in years gone by, and is today." Another soldier from Nebraska stated that he did "not approve of the course our government is pursuing with these people."[3]

Although many civilians also disapproved of the U.S. government's actions, the mood of the nation was generally in favor of imperialism. Numerous spokespeople advocated annexation of the Philippines as a way to gain wealth or to save "the little brown brother." Most agreed with President William McKinley that it was necessary to annex the Philippines "to educate the Filipinos and uplift and Christianize them."[4] One U.S. senator insisted that God had prepared "English-speaking and Teutonic peoples for a thousand years" to be "master organizers of the world" and to "administer government among savages and senile peoples."[5]

ACQUISITIONS AND INTERVENTIONS

The myth of white supremacy that helped push the nation into war with Spain brought not only territorial gains, but also spurred U.S. intervention in other nations' affairs. Although

Cuba gained its independence after the Spanish-American War, Puerto Rico, Wake Island, Guam, and eventually the Philippines came under U.S. rule. During the war the United States annexed Hawaii, primarily because the islands were strategically important to the war effort in the Pacific. In 1899 the United States and Germany partitioned the Samoan Islands, with the United States annexing the eastern portion.

Thus the United States had the beginnings of a Pacific empire. Many businesspeople and government officials believed there was now a secure gateway to markets in China.

The United States established an Open Door policy with China. The policy claimed to establish equal trading arrangements between China and the United States, Great Britain, Germany, Russia, and Japan. But Chinese dissidents, whom locals called Boxers (short for Fists of Righteous Harmony), wanted to oust all foreigners from their nation. The Boxers blamed foreigners for all of China's problems and laid siege to embassies in Peking in June 1900. This was called the Boxer Rebellion. An international army that included U.S. soldiers took over the embassies in August, and once the danger was over, the United States and Britain proclaimed their "natural supremacy."

That year, Theodore Roosevelt, who gained fame as a "Rough Rider" galloping to battle victories in Cuba, promoted imperialist ideas and was elected vice-president of the United States. When President McKinley was killed by a fanatic anarchist in 1901, Roosevelt became president. President Roosevelt soon issued, and often repeated, his now famous statement adapted from an African proverb: "Speak softly, and carry a big stick; you will go far."

Roosevelt used his "big stick" to push through plans proposed for decades to build a canal through the Colombian province of Panama that would connect the Atlantic and Pacific Oceans. The United States paid Colombia $10 million and leased a ten-mile-wide strip of land, called the Canal Zone, for $250,000 per year. The United States guaranteed Panama's independence in exchange for the Canal Zone. However, U.S. troops were stationed on the isthmus during construction and long afterward.

Building the Panama Canal was no simple matter. Construction began in 1904 and was completed in 1914 at a cost of millions of dollars and 22,000 lives. Most deaths were due to the same diseases that had plagued troops in the Spanish-American War: malaria and yellow fever. Following that war, Major Walter Reed led a medical team in Cuba that proved yellow fever was spread by infected mosquitoes. At the end of 1900, he wrote to his wife, rejoicing that he had been allowed "to do something good to alleviate human suffering."[6]

It fell to Major William Crawford Gorgas to apply Reed's theories. Even though Gorgas doubted that mosquitoes carried diseases, he effectively administered sanitation controls in Havana, Cuba, and eliminated mosquito breeding places, eggs, and larvae. His efforts helped wipe out the yellow fever scourge in that city by 1902 and later in the Panama Canal Zone. He is credited with the success of the canal construction, which was halted for a time because of the many deaths from yellow fever.

At the time the canal construction began, Roosevelt applied his intervention policies in the Dominican Republic, which had declared bankruptcy. European creditors threatened to use force to collect their debts from the Dominican Republic, so in 1904 Roosevelt took steps to stop such action. He set forth his Corollary to the Monroe Doctrine, as it became known.

The Monroe Doctrine, established in 1823, declared that European powers should not interfere in the politics of the Americas and that the United States, in turn, would not intrude in affairs of European nations. But in light of the European threat, Roosevelt in his Corollary said the United

States was justified in intervening "in flagrant cases" of wrongdoing. He said the nation should "exercise international police power." This principle allowed the United States to take over, by mutual agreement, the Dominican Republic's financial affairs, and its debts were repaid. But the Roosevelt Corollary was used later to justify forced interventions.

A "BIG STICK" ON THE DOMESTIC SCENE

Even though Roosevelt was often criticized and depicted as the world's policeman, he was also seen by some as a "progressive," a person advocating democratic reforms. Abuses of economic power and the numerous social problems brought on by industrialization prompted calls for regulation of U.S. business. The Sherman Anti-Trust Act of 1890 had done little to break up large corporations so that small firms could compete fairly in the marketplace.

Dozens of books and hundreds of newspaper and magazine articles attacked the powerful robber barons and demanded social justice. Writers of such works were labeled "muckrakers," a term first used by President Roosevelt to criticize the critics. These muckrakers, though, alerted the public to corruption and abuses of power by monopolies and crooked politicians, and galvanized efforts for change.

Roosevelt himself, who had promised a Square Deal for all sections of the nation, began efforts as soon as he became president to enforce antitrust laws and to restrict big business. He also helped settle a labor dispute in favor of workers.

In 1902 the United Mine Workers went on strike against coal companies, demanding increased wages, a shorter work day, and union recognition. Coal miners faced dreadful conditions and worked long hours. Average earnings were $560 per year, and most workers owed money to the company store for goods purchased on credit. "At the Markle Coal Company, twelve-year-old Andrew Chippie's forty cents a day was regularly credited against a debt left by his father, killed four years before in a mine accident," reported historian Walter Lord.[7]

After 140,000 miners walked off their jobs in May, owners shut down the mines. The walkout continued for months. Finally President Roosevelt called a conference to bring representatives of labor and mine owners together. When the owners refused to bargain, Roosevelt threatened to bring in the army to run the mines, which eventually brought about a strike settlement in October.

LABOR ORGANIZATION

From 1903 to 1917, when the United States entered World War I, union organizing increased. Some of the first unions formed in textile factories, where unhealthy and unsafe working conditions had changed little over the decades. Most of these unions consisted primarily of women, the majority of the textile workforce.

One of the first significant strikes by a women's labor union involved shirtwaist workers in New York and Philadelphia. Strikes in two shops began in September 1909 and continued for almost two months. But there was no large, general strike of textile workers. So on November 22 union organizers and workers gathered to determine what to do next. After numerous long speeches, Clara Lemlich, a teenage worker who had been through several strikes, asked to be heard. She addressed the crowd, saying:

> I am a working girl, and one of those who are on strike against intolerable conditions. I am tired of listening to speakers who talk in general terms. What we are here for is to decide whether or not we will strike. I offer a resolution that a general strike be declared—now![8]

The enthusiasm generated by Lemlich's speech resulted in a major strike of women workers that lasted until February 1910. The workers gained little, but they inspired workers in other industries—railroads, for example—to strike for better conditions.

REFORM MOVEMENTS IN THE "PROGRESSIVE ERA"

In the years before World War I, the United States not only became a world power but also a nation of reformers. Americans from all walks of life demanded that their country move forward in efforts to improve living and working conditions for the majority and to seek social justice. Presidents Theodore Roosevelt, William Howard Taft, and President Woodrow Wilson led during this period, which became known as the Progressive Era.

Among the numerous reforms were changes in the meatpacking, canning, and drug industries. Filthy conditions in meatpacking plants had been described in Upton Sinclair's novel *The Jungle*, and federal agents sent to Chicago to investigate found that meat was "shovelled from filthy wooden floors, piled on tables rarely washed, pushed from room to room in rotten box cars, in all of which processes it was in the way of gathering dirt, splinters, floor filth, and the expectoration [spit] of tuberculous and other diseased workers."[9]

The Meat Inspection Act of 1906 soon followed. The law set standards for sanitation and required inspection of meats. The Pure Food and Drug Act passed about the same time protected consumers from foods and drugs that were adulterated or harmful.

Other reform legislation included the Employers' Liability Act of 1906, which made employers liable for injuries to workers on the job. Minimum wage laws also were passed in a number of states between 1912 and 1914.

Child labor had long been a problem. Thousands of young girls between ten and twelve years old worked in textile plants in both the South and the North. Young boys were commonly employed in steel mills and mines.

A few states prohibited employment of children in factories but allowed child labor at home. In New York City tenements, for example, child labor was often used to manufacture clothing or artificial flowers. From October 1906 to April 1907, several consumer and child-protection organizations conducted a joint investigation of child labor conditions and in 1908 issued a report. The report cited a manufacturer of artificial flowers who gave out work to a family

> in whose tenement rooms flowers are made by six children, aged two and one-half, five, eight, ten, fourteen and sixteen years. In another family Angelo, aged fourteen years, cannot work legally in a factory until he reaches a higher grade in school, nor can he work at home during hours when school is in session, but his little sister Maria, aged three years, because she is not old enough to go to school and because the home work law contains no prohibition of child labor, may help her mother pull bastings and sew on buttons . . . . Many good citizens would demand the prosecution of a manufacturer who employed in his factory Tony aged four years, Maria aged nine, Rose aged ten, Louisa aged eleven, and Josephine aged thirteen years . . . . Yet the public has not raised an effective protest against the same employer when he turns these children's home into a branch of his factory.[10]

The public finally did react, however, due to the tireless work of reformers in such organizations as the National Child Labor Committee and its state and local groups. Articles in newspapers and magazines also appeared, demanding protection for young workers. Most states passed laws banning employment of underage children and limiting the working hours of older minors. But federal legislation protecting child workers did not come about until 1938 with passage of the Fair Labor Standards Act.

During the first decade of the twentieth century, women saw some gains in their political efforts to pass suffrage legislation. In six states women were allowed to vote in the presidential election of 1912. But passing an amendment to the U.S. Constitution guaranteeing women's right to vote was a much more difficult task. Those who worked for the cause were subjected to harassment, imprisonment, and threats on their lives.

The movement was overshadowed by the outbreak of World War I and bitter debates over whether the United States should remain neutral in the face of Germany's "warfare against mankind," as President Woodrow Wilson called it in a speech before Congress on April 2, 1917. He concluded his message with a summons to make the world "safe for democracy." By April 6, the United States was at war with Germany.

Breadlines were common during the Great Depression, which devastated the country in the 1930s. Many lost their jobs and homes and relied on charity for food.

6

THE AFTERMATH OF WORLD WAR I

I heard the band playing and loud shouting . . . . I knew the news had come that Germany had signed the armistice, whether official or otherwise. And, of course, I went out and added my voice to the general chorus. The band was marching in single file, and the whole camp seemed to be following, single file, hands on shoulders.[1]

This description of Armistice Day (now celebrated as Veterans Day), November 11, 1918, comes from the diary of George Nowel Lantz, who served in the U.S. Navy in England. Although a treaty was signed on November 11, the peace conference that was to finalize the treaty and the "war to end all wars" did not begin until January 18, 1919.

CREATING A PEACE PLAN

Twenty-seven victorious Allied powers were represented at the conference. The leaders were the heads of the Big Four powers: Woodrow Wilson of the United States, Georges Clemenceau of France, David Lloyd George of Britain, and Vittorio Orlando of Italy. They had been able to work side-by-side to end the hostilities, which had seen sixty-five million take up arms across Europe, ending the lives of over eight million of them and wounding twenty-one million others. But when it came time to create a peace plan, these leaders had very diverse ideas about what should be included.

President Wilson wanted to implement his Fourteen Points, a set of principles that he believed would establish a just and lasting peace for all involved. His plan had been the basis for the armistice that had ended the fighting, and its overall goal was to expand democracy. The principles included removing all barriers to trade; honoring freedom of the seas; ending secret diplomacy; and disarming. The most important point was the creation of an international body called the League of Nations to resolve disputes and provide cooperative security among all member nations against future aggression.

Lloyd George had no intention of allowing free passage on the seas, and he distrusted Wilson's idealism. Orlando expected to be repaid and to gain former German territories, which had been promised to Italy in exchange for joining the Allies. And Clemenceau was determined to exact revenge against its neighbor Germany for the devastation that cost France the lives of nearly 1.5 million of its citizens and close to $50 billion.

The only one of Wilson's points upon which the leaders agreed was establishing the League of Nations. This they did on January 25, 1918. The Supreme Council of the League, which was represented by the Big Four Allied powers and Japan, then spent three more months creating a compromise agreement, the Treaty of Versailles, that would officially end World War I.

On June 28, after months of a continuing naval blockade of their country, the German government signed the treaty under protest. This document required Germany to accept sole responsibility and guilt for the damage that had been done by the war. It also penalized the country by calling for huge reparations and imposing military and economic restrictions that were designed to keep Germany humbled and of little threat to her neighbors in the future.

While many can understand the need of European countries to punish the aggressors for the massive loss of life and the $282 billion cost of the war, history shows that the punitive approach was an absolute failure. In less than two decades, the stark conditions that had been imposed on Germany proved to be the perfect incubator for hatching the most diabolical plot for world domination. In many ways, Nazi dictator Adolf Hitler and World War II were the direct result of the Allies' rejection of Wilson's concept of "peace without victory."

A RETURN TO ISOLATION

When President Wilson returned to the United States, he found that the Republican-controlled Senate had no intention of ratifying the Treaty of Versailles or joining the League of Nations. The failure to win approval in the Senate devastated Wilson, who decided to take his case to the people. While touring the country to explain his concept for a lasting peace, he suffered a stroke on September 25, 1919, in Pueblo, Colorado. He never recovered, and the treaty was formally rejected in March 1920. The League remained a weak and ineffectual institution because the United States refused to join.

Many in the United States had been inspired to join the war because of Wilson's moral argument that victory would establish a secure world where nations could coexist in peace. The reality did not meet expectations.

The final straw for many was the year-long influenza outbreak that had started in Europe in 1917. Arriving in the

United States a year later, it eventually claimed five hundred thousand lives. The people were weary and disillusioned. The nation turned inward once again to confront the issues that were affecting lives on a daily basis.

CONFLICTING FORCES

During the first decade after the war, many conflicting forces were at work. On the economic front, the boom in production for the war effort had brought wage increases as prices for goods and services rose. But the economy soon cooled down. Old labor grievances that had not been resolved prior to the war again took center stage, and millions of workers struck for better conditions.

Unresolved social issues also created conflicts. When African-American men, for example, returned from the fighting in Europe, they possessed a new sense of freedom and power. But they immediately met resistance. Lynchings and other forms of racial violence increased. Black churches and sometimes entire black towns were burned to the ground, as was the case in Rosewood, Florida, a tragedy rarely mentioned until it became the basis for a 1997 film. A revitalized Ku Klux Klan terrorized black families that dared to exercise their rights as U.S. citizens. Race riots occurred in numerous big cities across the United States.

In more subtle ways, the New England establishment reacted to changes brought on by the influx of Catholic and Jewish immigrants who had arrived from Europe in the mass migrations around the turn of the century. Some white Protestants opposed organized labor that favored immigrant work forces, seeing them as threats. They also associated drinking with immigrant workers—the beer gardens of German neighborhoods, for example—and worked for adoption of the Eighteenth Amendment.

This 1919 amendment made it illegal to manufacture, sell, or transport alcoholic beverages in the United States, and the subsequent Volstead Act provided for enforcement of the ban. The Prohibition laws, however, were virtually ignored. Illegally manufactured or transported liquor was available almost everywhere and was known as "bootlegging," from the old method of carrying bottles next to the leg in a tall boot. A World War I veteran in St. Paul, Minnesota, recalled that

> if you'd go to a nightclub, you'd bring your bottle of liquor and set it by your chair, order a soft drink and pour in your liquor . . . . Of course, everybody made his own beer, usually in a 10-gallon crock. You'd put in distilled water, pour in stuff you could buy at the grocery store called Black Knight malt, let it stand for four or five days, then bottle it. We didn't feel we were lawbreakers.[2]

Selling bootleg liquor proved to be lucrative for many otherwise law-abiding citizens. It also attracted ruthless gangsters like Al Capone. His mob and others quickly built sophisticated networks of distilleries, bottling plants, and delivery routes to supply the demand for liquor at hidden bars known as "speakeasies," at legitimate restaurants, and even in neighborhood grocers. The end result was a general sense of lawlessness in many urban centers throughout the period, known as the Roaring Twenties or the Jazz Age. When it became obvious to enough legislators that Prohibition was causing more problems than solutions, the statutes were annulled by the Twenty-first Amendment. That 1933 amendment to the Constitution is the only amendment ever added to undo another amendment.

A long-standing conflict that was resolved not long after World War I was woman suffrage. For years, women, along with men who supported their cause, had lobbied, demonstrated, and agitated to pass an amendment to the Constitution guaranteeing women's right to vote. Women's new independence and political power brought about by their working outside the home during the war no doubt helped convince states to ratify the Nineteenth Amendment in 1920. The amendment states that the right of citizens to vote "shall not be denied or abridged by the United States or by any State on account of sex."

TECHNOLOGY AND PROGRESS

One of the obvious effects of the war in Europe was the development of technology to kill people at rates never before experienced. More advances in warfare were developed during World War I than in any other conflict before or since, although warfare technology certainly was enhanced in later years. One advance was the use of airplanes for controlled flight, as nations improved on the 1903 experiments of brothers Orville and Wilbur Wright.

Submarines and tanks also greatly influenced the outcome of the fighting. The newly improved submarine, for instance, helped the German navy undermine the dominance of the British global fleet and almost turned the tide of victory. Poison gas, the machine gun, and substantial improvements in artillery contributed to the beginning of mechanized (modern) warfare.

Perhaps of even greater importance was the application of the new field telephones and radio sets, which made immediate communication possible. Commanders operating at headquarters beyond firing lines could keep in constant touch with their units located in battlefields miles away.

These war-related technological developments created many new possibilities for the nation, as did the mass-production of the automobile, improved roads, the motion picture, and the expanded availability of electricity and the telephone. It was a time of creativity and reinvention.

Although the 1920s was a time of economic prosperity and technological progress, only a small minority of the people actually profited financially from the advances in industrial production. In the election of 1920, Warren Harding became president, winning in a landslide, and the balance of power shifted back to the Republican Party. For the remainder of that decade, big business had good friends in the White House.

Harding died in office in 1923 and Calvin Coolidge, the vice-president, became president. Throughout his tenure (1923-1929), Coolidge supported the private business sector and opposed reforms that might hinder investments and expansion of corporate interests. In his words, "The business of America is business."

Many business people speculated in stocks and real estate, driving prices to all-time highs. Common wage earners were not able to keep up with inflation—increases in prices of goods and services. Easy credit had put many workers into debt, and banks were failing at the rate of six hundred per year. Farmers, too, were suffering from a long-time decline in their profits.

Then in October 1929, the stock market crashed, launching the Great Depression.

Many workers had literally no way to earn a living. Changes in technology were eliminating their old jobs and new ones were not being created as fast. From 1929 to 1933, unemployment rose from 1.5 million to approximately fifteen million. At the peak of the Great Depression, one out of every four workers was unemployed. Families lost their homes and many became nomads, wandering from place to place looking for work. Among the homeless were about 250,000 young people.

Breadlines were a common site in many cities as unemployed workers and their families came to rely on soup kitchens and charities for their survival. Despite problems, one woman recalled that

> Some people were especially kind. I had small children, so the milkman said, "You need this; you've always paid and that's the way it's gonna be." He went to the company, and it said, "Fine." So we always had milk. But we all had to stand in line once a month to get food and clothes. Sometimes you'd get a couple of dozen eggs and bread and some kind of vegetable.[3]

By 1933 stocks were valued at only one-fifth of their 1930 levels. Eleven thousand banks had to close their doors because people were defaulting on their loans. Two billion dollars in bank deposits simply disappeared.

President Herbert Hoover, who succeeded Coolidge, had great faith in the forces of the market. In his view, the capitalist system would right the economy. Previous recessions, Hoover reasoned, had usually lasted only a year or two at most. But this economic slowdown was different. It was affecting industrial nations all over the world.

FDR'S NEW DEAL

President Hoover had built a respected reputation by helping millions of displaced Europeans find food and shelter before and after World War I. He was considered a great humanitarian. However, much of the blame for the continuing Depression was laid at his feet. In the election of 1932, Hoover lost to New York Governor Franklin Delano Roosevelt by a huge margin.

Roosevelt knew that the public was deeply frightened. He addressed the problem in his first inaugural speech, declaring that "the only thing we have to fear is fear itself." Unlike

Hoover, he tried to build confidence by showing that the government could make a difference and turn around the economy.

One of the most important aspects of Roosevelt's plan for recovery, called the New Deal, was providing jobs for desperate people. He and his wife, Eleanor Roosevelt, were deeply concerned about the young victims of the Depression. At the urging of the First Lady, President Roosevelt created federal youth agencies and programs that provided direct relief for young people. The Civilian Conservation Corps, for example, employed young men to work on conservation projects. Through the Federal Emergency Relief Administration, college students received work-study jobs to help them stay in school.

"The high degree of public attention the Roosevelt administration focused upon poverty and the problems of the younger generation, convinced many children and teens that the New Deal was on their side," according to Robert Cohen of the University of Georgia. Cohen's article on a World Wide Web site called the New Deal Network explains how "Mrs. Roosevelt's involvement in youth issues and relief efforts for the poor made a strong impression on many teens and children."[4]

Young people often wrote to Mrs. Roosevelt, asking in a somber and "adult-like tone" for help. One girl requested a bicycle because she desperately needed transportation to school. "The school which I attend is very far and as I am not very healthy I often get pains in my sides. My father only works for two days a week and there are six in my family, it is impossible in almost every way that I get a bicycle," she wrote.[5]

Others asked Mrs. Roosevelt for her "old soiled" dresses so they would have something to "ware to school," or funds to pay doctor bills or to buy food. The requests for personal help numbered in the tens of thousands and unfortunately could not possibly be fulfilled. But the First Lady staunchly supported New Deal programs for youth, which helped millions of teenagers gain employment, provided aid to dependent children, and financed numerous school programs.[6]

Although Roosevelt's recovery plan was inconsistent and in the end failed to achieve the economic turnaround he had hoped for, the New Deal established a role for government that had never before been tried in the United States. The programs that were initiated in those eight years were based on a principle that the federal government had a responsibility to protect its citizens, not just from enemies abroad, but from the consequences of greed and economic exploitation at home.

Many criticized Roosevelt's programs as "make work," but the nation benefited from the federal projects, which left a legacy of schools, airports, parks, and numerous other public facilities, as well as cultural works by writers, actors, musicians, and artists. Even Roosevelt's political enemies came to accept the new regulations that legalized union activity, established old-age insurance (Social Security), oversaw securities trading, and created unemployment compensation programs. Opponents have railed against the large bureaucracies that these programs created, but they have lasted successfully until the turn of the twenty-first century.

WAR IN EUROPE, AGAIN

The 1930s economic depression was even worse in other countries than in the United States. Germany was especially affected because it had never recovered from World War I and the sanctions imposed on it by the Allies. Political factions were polarized, the people were depressed and resentful, and Adolf Hitler's ideas started to make sense to many. He blamed Germany's problems on Jews, communism, and capitalism.

Appealing to their national and warrior spirit, Hitler gave Germans a way out of their ills. His party, the National Socialist Party (the Nazis), won a majority in Germany's Congress in 1931, and he was appointed to lead the country in 1933. Within five years he illegally annexed Austria. Czechoslovakia soon followed, and war erupted when England and France helped Poland fight an invasion of German troops in 1939.

Roosevelt had kept the United States out of the fighting until 1941, when a Japanese sneak attack on Pearl Harbor, a U.S. naval base in the Pacific, ended U.S. neutrality. Japan was Germany's ally and wanted to expand its empire in the Pacific. The massive industrialization that the United States underwent to supply the war effort quickly ended the Depression. Once more the country focused on a common goal: winning World War II and defeating fascism.

That war cost more than 290,000 American lives—a small number of deaths compared to the millions exterminated in Nazi concentration camps in Europe and the many more millions of Europeans and Asians killed in battle or in bombings of cities, towns, and villages. The aftermath of the second world war was even more unsettling than that of the first.

After World War II, Martin Luther King Jr. stirred the conscience
of the nation regarding its unfair civil rights policies.

7

IN THE SHADOW OF THE ATOMIC BOMB

"Born in this century, tempered by war, disciplined by a hard and bitter peace," is the way President John F. Kennedy described the post–World War II generation during his inaugural address in 1961. Many others have also tried before and since to summarize the period from 1945 through the 1950s and early 1960s. *Fortune* magazine called it "a dream era," a time of economic prosperity when people could buy goods and services that had not been available during the war. Purchases ranged from appliances, homes, and cars to television sets and frozen TV dinners.

The Servicemen's Readjustment Act of 1944, popularly known as the GI Bill, also helped stimulate the economy as the federal government spent billions of dollars to provide education, business and home loans, and medical treatment for World War II veterans.

The postwar period was a time to settle down and be comfortable in the suburbs, which grew rapidly with demands for new housing. Some thirteen million new homes were built between 1948 and 1958.[1] Women gave up factory and other paid work as men returning from the war took over their jobs. Marriages and families grew, and the baby boom generation (babies born between 1946 and 1964) came on the scene. From 1948 to 1957, when the baby boom peaked, the U.S. population increased by almost forty million.[2]

Many tried to conform to the idealized family life portrayed in books, magazines, newspapers, movies, and TV shows like *Father Knows Best* and *Ozzie and Harriet.* In this model life, women were expected to be career homemakers, raise the children, work with the school, and do volunteer work. They were expected to subordinate their own preferences to their family's. By doing otherwise, a woman risked being labeled a "sterilized feminist," "anti-God," or a "communist."

A kind of religious sanctimony prevailed at this time as well. Across the land preachers, teachers, political leaders, and other public figures encouraged piety. They denounced "godless communism" and "communist aggression" around the world. President Dwight Eisenhower proclaimed that "without God, there could be no American form of government, nor an American way of life."[3] In 1954 the phrase "one nation under God" was added to the Pledge of Allegiance, and the following year Congress passed legislation requiring that "In God We Trust" be placed on currency.

But records show that the 1950s were not simply a period of "Happy Days," as many believed. Numerous people began to criticize a culture that valued conformity over individuality and creativity. Critics also denounced a society that continued to suppress and deny the civil rights of African Americans and other minorities. In addition, there was a pervasive fear throughout the United States that communism would take over the world, which led to the persecution of thousands of American citizens and immigrants thought to be communists or communist sympathizers. Anticommunism and conflicts over civil rights upset the serene exterior of the post–World War II era.

THE BOMB

The fighting in Europe ended in May 1945 with Germany's surrender. Harry S. Truman, who became president when Franklin Roosevelt died in 1945, ordered the atomic (nuclear) bombing of the Japanese cities of Hiroshima and Nagasaki in August 1945. The Japanese surrendered, and a peace treaty was signed on September 2, bringing World War II to an end.

Though the world rejoiced that the fighting was over, many had mixed emotions about the bombings. One elderly woman recalled that she felt "consternation and sorrow and relief that the war was over." She explained "I didn't hold President Truman at fault for dropping the bomb, because there was so much to be said for saving of lives of Americans. But it also seemed evil."[4]

Thousands of innocent Japanese citizens certainly experienced the evil of the bomb. Masako Okawa, who was eight years old when the bomb fell on Nagasaki, lost her mother and two sisters to the effects of nuclear radiation. Masako was buried under the rubble of her home and was terribly scarred from injuries she suffered. In later years, she reported,

> After graduating from junior high school, I began to notice the appearance of symptoms of the dread atomic disease: periodic nausea, low blood pressure, hypersensitivity to cold, internal hemorrhage, and purple spots on my arms and legs. Though the spots disappeared, they usually returned in a few days to inspire me with horror of the day when my entire body would be covered with them and I would die.[5]

To this day, the science that created the bomb has failed to find a cure for the terrible effects of nuclear radiation.

In the United States after the war, many feared that the

bomb could some day destroy their own cities and towns. Congress passed the Atomic Energy Act in 1946, which set up a civilian commission to control the use of uranium and plutonium, the materials used in nuclear bombs. The act also required the commission to encourage the development of peaceful uses for atomic energy.

Nevertheless, nuclear destruction threatened. When bombs were tested in the Pacific, the deadly radioactive fallout was measured 150 miles away. Many people believed that Armageddon—the end of the world—was at hand, and some families built underground shelters in the false hope that they would be protected from a nuclear blast. These shelters were equipped with canned goods, bottled water, sleeping bags, and other survival gear, including, in some cases, a shotgun to keep out intruders. Although only fifteen hundred shelters were built in the 1950s, the number increased to at least two hundred thousand by 1961 when the possibility of another world war seemed on the horizon.[6]

CONTAINING COMMUNISM

Along with the threat of nuclear annihilation was the problem of how to stop the spread of communism. Soviet Premier Joseph Stalin established socialist states in Eastern Europe and in 1947 hoped to take over Greece, Turkey, and other countries whose economies were devastated by the war. President Truman called for a U.S. policy to fend off communist aggression by shoring up European countries. He advocated supporting people who were resisting attempts to be ruled by armed minorities. His policy became known as the Truman Doctrine. The rivalry between communist and noncommunist nations, along with the nuclear arms race, developed after World War II and was known as the Cold War.

Congress passed a financial aid bill for Greece and Turkey to help them gain economic stability. Other European nations also needed help, although some aid had come from the United Nations (UN). This world organization was planned in 1944 and created in 1945 with the aim of preserving peace and improving living conditions worldwide. But UN aid was not enough to save the economies of Western Europe, and in 1947 Secretary of State George Marshall suggested a European Recovery Program, called the Marshall Plan, to prevent "hunger, poverty, desperation, and chaos"—conditions likely to foster communism. The Marshall Plan also helped assure that the United States would have trading partners and markets for goods in the years ahead. Launched in 1948, the program spent $13.3 billion over four years to rebuild Europe and $2.3 billion to reconstruct Japan's cities and economy.[7]

Yet communism was still a threat in Asia and Europe. Germany and the city of Berlin had been divided among the four Allies: Great Britain, France, the Soviet Union, and the United States. But in 1948 the western portion of Germany, including the western half of Berlin, was organized under a separate federal government and eventually became known as the Federal Republic of Germany, or West Germany. The Soviets, who occupied the eastern portion of Germany, wanted to bring Berlin under communist control and tried to prevent the formation of a separate West Germany. They blocked traffic going in and out of West Berlin, cutting off food, coal, and other basic necessities.

The Berlin blockade did not succeed, however. The United States Air Force, with the help of Great Britain's Royal Air Force, France, and West Berlin leaders, came to the aid of the city's people with airlifts of food and equipment. Although there were some crashes and deaths due to storms and poor landing conditions, casualties were low, and lifesaving supplies were delivered on a daily basis beginning in June 1948. The Soviets lifted the blockade in mid-May 1949, but the airlift continued until September.

In 1994 Secretary of State Warren Christopher, speaking in West Berlin, paid tribute to the great achievement of the airlift that "delivered more than 2 million tons of supplies to Berlin." But, Christopher emphasized,

> equally impressive in the eyes of the world was the courage and resilience of Berliners—braving hunger, cold, and darkness so that freedom would prevail.
>
> . . . Despite their deprivation, Berliners gave the fliers the best that they had: books, cigarette lighters, flowers, and prayers. And . . . the fliers gave their best to the Berliners in return.
>
> . . . One 15-year old girl wrote of the casualties of the airlift. "Their sacrifice," she said, "reminds us that in this world there are higher things than national egoism—namely, humanity and the existence of all peoples in human dignity."[8]

After the blockade ended, the eastern zone of Germany came under communist rule and was called the German Democratic Republic, dividing the nation. Even though fighting did not break out during the blockade, the potential for violence was ever-present.

Later, in 1961, East Germany built a wall sealing off the east-west borders of Berlin. It was built to stop the steady stream of refugees fleeing to West Berlin. This infamous wall stayed in place for twenty-eight years, until 1989.

Such conflicts with no armed combat were part of the Cold War against communism that lasted until 1992.

The Cold War was not confined just to Europe. After World War II, communists organized in China and other parts of Asia. Korea, which had been divided at the end of the war, became two separate entities in 1948, with communists gaining power in the northern region. When communist forces invaded South Korea in 1950, the United States became involved in what was called a "police action" to stop the communists without engaging in armed conflict. However, the United States military soon entered the war against North

Korea, which lasted for three years and preserved the independence of South Korea.

ANTICOMMUNIST FRENZY AND McCARTHYISM

A House Un-American Activities Committee (HUAC) had been in operation to investigate suspected communists since 1938, but after World War II, an anticommunist hysteria prevailed in the United States. President Truman in 1947 signed an executive order, setting up a program to investigate government employees and determine their loyalty to the United States. Thousands were investigated, but no communists were found. The U.S. Congress also passed, over Truman's veto, the McCarran Internal Security Act of 1950, requiring communist or so-called communist-front organizations to register with the attorney general. Two years later, Congress passed the McCarran-Walter Act, which required loyalty checks for visiting foreigners and allowed the attorney general to deport immigrants—even those who had become citizens—who were suspected of being members of communist groups.

As the anticommunist fever rose, Alger Hiss, who had once worked in the federal government, was accused of spying for the Soviet Union during the 1930s. Hiss sued his accuser, Whittaker Chambers, for libel but was himself convicted of lying to HUAC and sentenced to a five-year prison term. He was not tried on espionage charges because the statute of limitations protected him—he could not be tried for a crime allegedly committed years before.

In another widely publicized case, Julius and Ethel Rosenberg were arrested and convicted of sending atomic bomb secrets to the Soviet Union. The Rosenbergs always proclaimed their innocence, but they were executed in 1953 even though others found guilty of spying were sentenced only to jail terms. Many people today still believe the Rosenbergs were framed because of an anticommunist hysteria. However, evidence released in 1995 shows that Julius Rosenberg was part of a Soviet spy ring, although there is no proof that he passed on significant information about the atomic bomb.[9]

Senator Joseph R. McCarthy of Wisconsin led the pack of those eagerly searching for communists in every walk of life. McCarthy exploited the nation's anxieties about the communist threat, and from 1950 to 1954 he charged that communists were everywhere in the federal government. But his charges were false.

McCarthy "lied vividly and with bold imagination; he lied, often, with very little pretense of telling the truth," as one commentator noted.[10] These tactics, known as McCarthyism, began to backfire when he took on the U.S. Army.

For more than a month in 1954 the U.S. Senate held televised Army–McCarthy hearings, which showed McCarthy treating witnesses rudely and claiming to have evidence of communists in government. No such evidence ever appeared, however, and the public soon saw what a bully McCarthy was. One couple who listened to the hearings on radio and watched them on television recalled that they "cheered with joy" when McCarthy was undone. For the first time they realized that an elected official could "destroy the careers and lives of innocent citizens."[11] The Senate condemned McCarthy, and by the end of 1954 he was no longer an influence in Congress.

BATTLING DISCRIMINATION

While much of the country was caught up in the "red scare," many African Americans in the United States were trying to gain equality. Black veterans of World War II as well as African Americans who had supported the war effort at home had fought and worked to establish democracy and to eliminate white supremacy. They no longer would accept segregation and discrimination in schools, public facilities, businesses, and workplaces.

Although President Eisenhower pressed for civil rights in the federal government, and some facilities like veterans hospitals were desegregated, he did not get involved in what he considered state matters, such as school integration. But during the early 1950s there were numerous challenges to public school segregation.

In 1954 the U.S. Supreme Court handed down a decision in *Brown v. Board of Education of Topeka, Kansas,* which declared that public schools should be desegregated "with all deliberate speed." A few all-white schools in the South complied, although they did so by allowing only a few blacks into the schools, but in many instances southern school systems defied the law. Violence often accompanied attempts by African Americans to enroll in all-white schools.

When a federal court ordered that black students be enrolled in Central High School in Little Rock, Arkansas, in 1957, Governor Orval Faubus called out the National Guard to keep blacks out. President Eisenhower sent one thousand paratroopers from the 101st Airborne Division to enforce the federal order and protect African American students. White racists in the school threatened to lynch the black students and often physically attacked them.

After the federal government recalled the paratroopers, the Arkansas National Guard, which had kept the black students out of the school, was in charge. The "troops turned a blind eye" and "we were left to protect ourselves," wrote Melba Patillo Beals, one of the black students. She was a junior at Central High during that frightening time, and years later she wrote an article for *Cosmopolitan* magazine describing the numerous threats and indignities she suffered. One day she arrived at her school homeroom to see "a doll that resembled me, with a rope around her neck, hanging from the door frame." In another instance she found peanut butter laced with glass on her desk seat. She was also attacked by a white bully with a switchblade who slashed through the cover of a book she held up to protect herself, while a guardsman merely looked on "with a twisted smile."

Though she completed her junior year, Melba and the other students were unable to reenter Central High at the beginning of the next school term. Governor Faubus closed all of the Little Rock high schools for a year. By September 1959, "the unrest in Little Rock and the bounty on our heads . . . forced two of our seven families to move their homes away from that city forever," Beals wrote. "NAACP officials sent an announcement to chapters across the country, asking for families that would volunteer to give us safe harbor and support us in finishing our education." In 1960 the NAACP's legal arm forced Central High School to reopen as an integrated school.[12]

MORE CIVIL RIGHTS EFFORTS

The battle for civil rights in the postwar period included efforts to integrate numerous other public facilities. The now-famous bus boycott in Montgomery, Alabama, was initiated in 1955 when Rosa Parks, a seamstress, refused to give up her seat on a bus after a hard day at work to a white man who demanded that she move and go to the rear, as required by a racist city law. Parks was forced off the bus and arrested. The minister of Parks' church, the Reverend Martin Luther King Jr., called for a peaceful protest: a citywide boycott of the bus system. Despite threats, arrests, and firebombings of their homes, African Americans in Montgomery refused to ride on public buses for more than a year. In November 1956 the U.S. Supreme Court ruled that bus segregation was illegal.

The civil rights movement became a driving force against segregation and involved whites as well as African Americans.

Throughout the rest of the decade African Americans made additional strides toward equality. The Voting Rights

Act, the first civil rights act since the days of Reconstruction, was passed in 1957, authorizing the Justice Department to file lawsuits on behalf of blacks who had been denied their right to vote. More public facilities such as city swimming pools were integrated.

By the early 1960s, a "sit-in" movement began to desegregate lunch counters and other eating places. In 1962 Congress passed the Twenty-fourth Amendment, ratified in 1964, banning poll taxes as a requirement for voting. (Many blacks, as well as poor whites, could not afford the tax, thus had been kept from voting.) That year another civil rights act became law, banning discrimination in public housing and any programs that received federal funds.

These civil rights gains were often met with white backlash—murders of civil rights workers, bombings of black churches, and countless beatings and arrests. Still the march toward freedom went on. Sometimes it was led by enraged black-power advocates who thought white violence should be met with black violence. Angry confrontations erupted over segregated housing, schooling, jobs, and police brutality. And riots broke out in several major cities. Yet the black-power movement also spawned black pride and slogans like "black is beautiful."

At the same time, the nonviolent civil rights movement continued to press forward through the efforts of such organizations as the Southern Christian Leadership Conference, the NAACP, the Congress of Racial Equality, the Student Non-Violent Coordinating Committee, and the Urban League. These groups and leaders from various religious and community organizations and unions, as well as ordinary citizens, organized a huge march on Washington to dramatize African-American demands for equality. On August 28, 1963, more than 250,000 demonstrators, black and white, converged on the Lincoln Memorial where they heard Martin Luther King Jr. deliver his now-famous "I Have a Dream" speech.

The Vietnam War Memorial speaks silently yet eloquently of those who died in a conflict that polarized U.S. citizens. At the end of the war, the nation healed very slowly.

8

A Shell-Shocked Society

"In a sense we've come to our nation's capital to cash a check," King said in his speech at the Lincoln Memorial. He noted:

> When the architects of our Republic wrote the magnificent words of the Constitution and the Declaration of Independence, they were signing a promissory note to which every American was to fall heir. This note was a promise that all men—yes, black men as well as white men—would be guaranteed the unalienable rights of life, liberty, and the pursuit of happiness. It is obvious today that America has defaulted on this promissory note insofar as her citizens of color are concerned. Instead of honoring this sacred obligation, America has given the Negro people a bad check, a check which has come back marked "insufficient funds."[1]

Yet King, as his words convey, held out hope that his dream would be realized. "I have a dream," he said "that my four little children will one day live in a nation where they will not be judged by the color of their skin but by the content of their character." He inspired countless African Americans and others to work toward that dream.

But the 1960s was also a decade in which the United States was embroiled in numerous crises. The possibility of all-out nuclear war was never closer than during the Cuban missile crisis in 1962. The Soviet Union had built a missile base in Cuba, a nation headed by communist dictator Fidel Castro. The weapons could strike within three minutes, and they posed a real threat to heavily populated areas in two-thirds of the United States. President Kennedy demanded that the missiles be removed.

As the two superpowers faced off, another world war seemed on the horizon. However, the missiles were withdrawn, and a new era of negotiation between the USSR and the United States was eventually established.

Then the nation was numbed by the assassination of the much-loved John F. Kennedy in Dallas, Texas, on November 22, 1963. Vice-president Lyndon Johnson became president. Johnson had to deal with the unrest of the civil rights movement and other domestic problems. Soon he was also faced with the growing discontent over the U.S. involvement in Vietnam.

DISILLUSIONMENT

Most of the country had lived in unprecedented comfort and stability during the economic boom years following World War II. People did not understand what was happening just a few years removed from that golden era. The prospect of violence seemed to be everywhere. In reality it was never farther away than the nightly TV news.

The Vietnam War was the first conflict ever fought by the United States in which people had a front row seat to watch battlefield violence via their family's television set. The graphic displays, accompanied by lengthy reports and investigations, helped to turn popular opinion against a war that seemed to have no clear objectives. The need to "halt world communist aggression" did not inspire thousands of young men when their draft notices came in the mail. Burning draft cards became a popular protest action. Many went further—they left the country to avoid taking part in the war or went to jail.

Students were among the first to oppose the war, organizing peace marches and teach-ins. Mothers and fathers of draftees, loyal veterans of World War II and the Korean conflict, and others in the mainstream also began to question the motives of their government. Had policy makers in Washington, D.C., miscalculated the risks? Did they underestimate the genius and tenacity of the North Vietnamese leadership and its guerrilla army? Why should the U.S. support an unpopular regime in Southeast Asia, anyway? Wasn't this really an internal struggle, a Vietnam civil war?

There had been antiwar sentiment for each of the U.S. conflicts in the past, of course, but the breadth and fervor of the Vietnam peace movement was extraordinary. As the body count increased (fifty-eight thousand Americans and up to three million Vietnamese were killed in the conflict), and the bill mounted ($150 billion for the United States), critics became more and more numerous and vocal.

As protests moved into the streets all across the nation, President Lyndon Johnson's long and distinguished political career became one more casualty of the war. The outcry against escalating U.S. involvement in a war that appeared unwinnable forced Johnson out of the 1968 presidential race. Vice-President Hubert Humphrey received the Democratic nomination.

Richard Nixon, the Republican nominee, defeated Humphrey in a backlash against the Vietnam War and the more liberal domestic policies of Kennedy and Johnson. Johnson's support for the 1965 Voting Rights Act eliminated all qualifying tests for voter registration of blacks in the South. In addition, his Great Society and War on Poverty programs expanded the role of the federal government. Many programs that are accepted today in the United States, such as the Peace Corps, Medicare, Head Start, the Clean Air Act, the Water Quality Act, and public housing assistance, are the result of the Kennedy and Johnson view that government should be active on behalf of its citizens.

The cost of fighting a war halfway around the globe and maintaining liberal domestic programs proved to be far too expensive, however. The government had to borrow money to pay its bills, causing inflation, which was to remain a problem in the United States for thirteen more years.

President Nixon had little sympathy for the Great Society programs, and although he promised he had a "secret plan" to end the Vietnam War during his election campaign, his Vietnam War policies brought much the same results as that of his predecessor.

Throughout his first term Nixon held to a course of "Vietnamization," which was designed to gradually move the responsibility for the defense of South Vietnam to the Vietnamese army. He promised in the spring of 1970 to bring 150,000 U.S. troops home from Vietnam, but after this pledge he ordered the invasion of Cambodia. As a result, there was an explosion of protests across the United States.

At this time, an increasing number of Americans began to demand voting rights for eighteen-year-olds, reasoning that young people old enough to fight and die in a war ought to have the right to vote for the leaders who send them into battle. As a direct result of the Vietnam War, the Twenty-sixth Amendment was ratified in 1971, establishing the right of U.S. citizens "18 years of age, or older," to vote. Two years later, the draft was ended.

Body bags carrying dead GIs continued to arrive in the states. Finally, after much delay at the bargaining table, a peace treaty was signed in January 1973 and the United States withdrew from Vietnam.

The war was over, but not for many who took part in the battles or witnessed the death and destruction in Vietnam. Barbara Gluck, who worked as a photojournalist during the war and photographed numerous scenes of pain, hopelessness, and death, said, "When I came back from Vietnam I would describe my emotional state as catatonic. I couldn't work, I barely could move. I sat most of the time staring out windows. The intensity of my experiences in Vietnam rolled by so quickly that there wasn't time to absorb them until I returned."[2]

The U.S. forces never lost a major battle in the long years of the Vietnam conflict, but there was no doubt that they had lost the war.

The war had been fought to prevent the "domino effect"—one Asian country after another falling under communist domination. In the end, though, the communists controlled Vietnam, Laos, and Cambodia. Historian George Brown Tindall noted:

> The war described as a noble crusade on behalf of democratic ideals instead suggested that democracy was not easily transferable to Third World regions that lacked any historical experience with liberal values and representative government. The war designed to serve as a showcase for American military power instead eroded respect for the military so thoroughly that many young Americans came to regard military service as corrupting and ignoble.[3]

The country was so divided by its involvement in the conflict that the men and women who returned from the fighting in the final years were rarely given the respect and honor that veterans of other wars had received. Some became embittered and thought the war was not only a mistake but also "fundamentally, perhaps pathologically, evil," as U.S. Marine Corps veteran W. D. Ehrhart put it. Ehrhart explained that he paid for his part in that mistake with

> more than a decade of nightmares and alcohol and self-loathing; a white-hot fury, shapeless and unpredictable, that seared anyone who came too close; a loneliness profound as the silence between the stars. And I was lucky . . . . I have friends who were dumped into wheelchairs at 19 and won't be taken out again until they are loaded into their coffins. I have friends who still can't see an Asian face without trembling . . . .[4]

When soldiers came home, they were sometimes jeered at and spat upon by those who equated their actions with the mistakes of their government. A Vietnam veteran could even be an embarrassment to his family and friends. For veteran Walter McDougall, it was "as if my presence were a judgment upon the hawks who made me go and the doves who ducked having to go. It was as if Vietnam veterans were both morally superior and morally inferior to everyone else, at the same time."[5]

Veterans were an easy scapegoat for the guilt and anger that many Americans felt. The country did not know how to deal with defeat, something that had never happened to the United States in war. People were wary of any further foreign entanglements for many years to come. "No more Vietnams" was a phrase that became popular on the floor of Congress and in newspaper editorials.

It took nearly ten years from the end of the war for the healing process to begin at home. One of the first visible symbols of reconciliation was a massive V-shaped wall bearing the names of U.S. service men and women killed in the war; it was dedicated in Washington, D.C., November 13, 1982. The Vietnam Veterans Memorial, designed by Maya Yang Lin, belatedly honored those who had done their duty in the most unpopular war in the nation's memory.

A number of veterans continued to have problems integrating back into society, but this wall proved to be of immense help for some in putting the war behind them. As many visitors to the memorial have noted, people seem compelled to touch the wall. Wrote Larry Heinemann,

> Some touch it with their fingertips. Some lean into it with their fists. Some sweep their hands across it, as if stroking a horse's neck. Some visitors seem to embrace it.[6]

Another visitor noted, "For those who come [to the memorial], there is almost always a need to tell the story of a familiar name they find inscribed there."[7]

A Loss of Trust

The Vietnam era was the time when the baby boom generation started to come of age. Many from this group, born in the years just after the Second World War, began to question their parents' traditional ideals. Hippies and "radicals" started to dominate the headlines with stories of unbridled drug use, free love, and communal living experiments. Many of the "long-haired, tie-dyed" generation wanted nothing more than to drop out of the system. Others urged society to re-evaluate itself and to change practices that had gone unchallenged from the earliest days of the republic.

Sexuality and women's issues became more visible. Race relations came front and center as Dr. King and many others called for equality. Hispanics and Native Americans also organized to seek opportunities and justice for all people of color.

Then in April 1968 Martin Luther King was gunned down, killed while standing on the balcony of a motel in Memphis, Tennessee. His assassination sparked riots in more than sixty U.S. cities. Just two months later Senator Robert F. Kennedy was shot and killed by Sirhan Sirhan, a Palestinian who hated Kennedy's support of Israel.

These violent deaths and the turbulence of the decade were proof to many that the union was coming apart. In addition, the public had come to realize that its government had not told them the whole truth about why the United States was engaged in the Vietnam War and had misrepresented the progress of the war.

Then came a major political scandal. News broke about a break-in at Democratic National Committee headquarters at the Watergate complex in Washington, D.C., on June 17, 1972. Five burglars, hired by operatives of the Committee to Re-elect the President (CRP), were caught trying to steal information that could be used against George McGovern, the Democratic candidate for president in the upcoming election.

After Nixon was reelected in a landslide, investigative reporters from the *Washington Post* began a series of articles that linked the burglars' activity beyond CRP, to the Central Intelligence Agency and even the White House. A Senate investigative committee was convened in February 1973 to look into "what the President knew, and when he knew it."

For months the American people watched the live broadcast from the Senate hearing room as witness after witness testified to the inner workings of the Nixon presidency. It soon became clear that the president knew a great deal about the Watergate affair and that he and his closest advisors had attempted to cover up White House involvement in the debacle.

In late July 1974 the House Judiciary Committee, which had been investigating evidence of illegal White House activities, recommended that President Nixon be impeached on three separate charges: abuse of power, obstruction of justice, and defying committee subpoenas. With evidence mounting against him, Nixon realized that the House would vote to impeach him, and the Senate was ready to convict.

Richard Nixon addressed the nation on television on August 8, 1974, announcing that he would resign the next day and turn the presidency over to Gerald Ford, the vice-president. Thus he became the only man in U.S. history to resign from the highest office in the land. A month later, President Ford pardoned Nixon for any and all crimes that he may have committed while president. He did this, he said, so that the country could get back to normal after the nightmare of the Watergate affair.

UNEASE IN THE NATION

The national reaction was more a numbing of the senses than one of outrage. Historians point to this time as the turning point for many citizens in regard to their attitude toward government and politics. Polls showed lack of respect and an outright hostility toward those who would govern. There was—and still is—a general belief that government is corrupt and that most politicians are of low moral character.

Although President Ford and President Jimmy Carter, who won election in 1976, were decent, honorable men, they could do little to change the general uneasiness in the nation. Problems beyond the control of both presidents persisted. The price of oil purchased from the Organization of Petroleum Exporting Countries (OPEC) in the Middle East soared during the 1970s, increasing the prices on heating oil, gasoline, and electricity in the United States. This helped produce what became known as "stagflation"—the economy stagnated and prices inflated.

In 1979 the Ayatollah Ruhollah Khomeini, an Islamic leader, overthrew the government of the shah of Iran. The ayatollah made no secret of his hatred for the United States, which many Iranians shared. When President Carter invited the shah of Iran to come to the United States for cancer treatments, some Iranians were livid. With support from the Iranian government, a mob seized the U.S. embassy in Teheran and captured diplomats and staff, holding fifty-two people hostage for more than a year. The hostage crisis and stagflation contributed to Carter's defeat in the 1980 election. When Republican Ronald Reagan, an actor-turned-politician, became president, the Iranians released the hostages. Americans hoped that better days were at hand.

Reagan's friendly, persuasive manner made people feel good about themselves, their country, and their government. Even people who disagreed with Reagan's policies appreciated his easy-going ways and quick wit. He was especially admired for his courage after he was shot by a deranged John Hinckley and still managed to maintain his humor, reportedly joking to his wife, "Honey, I forgot to duck."[8]

Despite his charm, some of Reagan's programs and ideas were highly controversial, and today people still hotly debate the merits of his presidency. One debate is carried on through a homepage on the Internet where one side claims that Reagan freed the United States from overregulation by government and that his policies stimulated economic growth. The other side contends that Reagan was responsible for "8 years of unconscionable consumption, preposterous weapons procurement and unprecedented budget deficits which will burden America for decades."[9]

Once Reagan took office, he and his administration began to downsize the federal government and to spark economic growth through "supply-side" or "trickle-down" economic policies. According to this theory, government cuts taxes, particularly for the rich, who in turn invest their savings in business. As a result, more jobs are created, which provides more total revenue for government and greater prosperity for all citizens. His policies, called "Reaganomics," proved partially successful, but only after a terrible period of unemployment and recession in 1981 and 1982.

When prices stabilized and economic activity began to accelerate in 1983, rich people and some middle class families benefited. However, those in rural areas and the hard-hit midwestern states saw little change in their fortunes. Eight million more citizens joined the ranks of the poor, and statistics showed one out of every seven citizens was living below the official poverty line.

President Reagan's policies also relied heavily on borrowing to finance government activity. The yearly budget deficit reached $150 billion to $200 billion a year, more than twice what it had ever been. Much of the spending increases were for the military.

Nevertheless, President Reagan's popularity remained very high. His emphasis on traditional family values and commitment to a strong United States in foreign affairs appealed to a broad cross section of the electorate. In 1984 he was returned to office handily.

Reagan's agenda included not only increased defense spending but also attempts to stop what he viewed as the spread of world communism. He referred to the Soviet Union as the "evil empire," and during his two terms sent arms and the military to ward off Soviet aggression in Central America and on the island of Grenada. Some historians contend that Reagan's anticommunist efforts played a major role in ending the Cold War between the United States and the Soviet Union.

During his second term, Reagan met several times with the leader of the Soviet Union, Mikhail Gorbachev. Both men sought to lessen the rivalry that had been the centerpiece of both countries' foreign policies for years. In the latter part of the 1980s, most observers agreed that the Soviet system was bankrupt. Mikhail Gorbachev was desperate to create a new government for his country.

The repercussions within the USSR were volatile, and the United States stayed on alert. But by the end of the 1980s the breakup of the old Union of Soviet Socialist Republics was accomplished with very little bloodshed, and the Cold War ended in early 1990. The new U.S. president, George Bush, elected in 1988 to succeed and carry on Reagan's policies, could declare that the United States had won.

Victorious American forces head home through smoke from oil
fires set by defeated Iraqis. The smoke, which seriously polluted
the air over a widespread area, was an immediate aftermath of
the Persian Gulf War.

9

AFTER THE COLD WAR

"With the demise of the Soviet Union and the end of the Cold War, the world has begun to move away from that dangerous state of affairs," said Secretary of Defense William Perry on March 1, 1995, while testifying before the U.S. Senate's Foreign Relations Committee. Perry explained that by reducing nuclear weapons, the former Soviet Union had "contributed greatly to U.S. security." But he warned,

> The Russian arsenal remains the only force capable of threatening U.S. national survival. Furthermore, the spread of nuclear and other weapons of mass destruction now poses a larger and growing threat to U.S. and global security. The former Soviet Union is a potential source of nuclear material for states eager to develop their own nuclear capability. We must avoid a return to the large arsenals of the Cold War and prevent proliferation of such weapons.[1]

When the Soviet Union dissolved and the Cold War ended, the United States became the only remaining superpower on earth. Some argued that Japan was equal to, or above, the United States in terms of economic capability and capitalist growth, but no one disputed the strength of the U.S. military or the nation's substantial influence worldwide. President Bush was able to demonstrate U.S. military strength not long after he took office.

On August 2, 1990, Iraqi President Saddam Hussein ordered his armed forces to invade Kuwait, a small kingdom holding vast oil reserves. Leaders worldwide feared that Saddam Hussein would use that oil to control the international supply, which would throw world markets into chaos and deplete the wealth of national economies. To counteract that threat, President Bush created a "new world order," a coalition of thirty-one countries that were willing to send troops and arms to the Middle East to confront Hussein's aggression. These countries and others pledged $58 billion to support the war effort.

After the Iraqi leader refused to heed an ultimatum to withdraw his forces by January 15, 1991, President Bush ordered an air attack on the capital city of Baghdad the following day. This was the beginning of the Persian Gulf War, or Operation Desert Storm. The ground war began February 24. Only a few days later, on February 28, Hussein gave up, and Kuwait's independence was restored.

The swift and decisive victory had an immediate effect on Americans; they could put the defeat of Vietnam behind them. With the Iraqi devastation, the United States was finally able to reassert its "number one" position in world affairs. But those who fought in the war and families of Gulf War veterans have had mixed emotions about the aftermath of the war. As Jackie Olsen, who founded a group called Desert Storm Mom, wrote:

> I was happy when the Gulf War ended in victory in early 1991. As a mother, I was overjoyed that two of my sons, Scott and Tom, who fought in the war, were coming home. It never occurred to me that for my sons and thousands of other Gulf vets, the war was far from over.[2]

GULF WAR SYNDROME

Along with Scott and Tom Olsen, tens of thousands of Gulf War veterans have complained about illnesses that as yet have only been identified as the "Gulf War syndrome." Many believe they suffer from the effects of exposure to chemicals or biological weapons. Veterans in the United States as well as in Canada and European countries have reported debilitating health problems ranging from chronic fatigue and headaches to neuromuscular ailments and memory loss. But frequently the Gulf veterans have been told that their illnesses are due to war stress or are imagined.

For several years after the war, U.S. military officials insisted that no troops had been exposed to chemical attacks, but in 1995 they finally admitted that thousands of soldiers may have been exposed to low levels of poison, such as the nerve gas Sarin. However, officials declared there was "no credible evidence" that low-level exposure could produce the kind of symptoms suffered by Gulf War veterans.[3]

Several U.S. congressional committees and the National Institutes of Health (NIH) began to investigate the veterans' complaints. The NIH concluded that the illnesses were linked to the Gulf War, and legislation was passed to increase funds for research on the Gulf War Syndrome.

In May 1995 President Clinton appointed an Advisory

Committee on Gulf War Veterans' Illnesses, and in September the panel charged that the Pentagon and Department of Veterans Affairs (VA) had not "seriously attempted to educate veterans about the health effects of service in the Gulf War." According to the *New York Times*, the panel "accused the Defense Department of making a 'superficial' investigation of whether chemical or biological agents were released in the war."[4] Other critics have also charged that the Central Intelligence Agency (CIA) has covered up evidence showing that Iraq used chemical weapons against troops in the Gulf.

All of these charges have been denied, and Dr. Stephen Joseph, the Pentagon's top health official, told *Newsweek* magazine that there is no doubt veterans "are experiencing real symptoms and illnesses with real consequences." But he believes that politics is now overwhelming science in this issue.[5]

As the political debate over the Gulf War syndrome goes on, scientists continue to look for clear answers to veterans' health problems. According to a report in *American Medical News*, the majority of Gulf vets with ailments "have been diagnosed with known illnesses . . . and have received or are receiving appropriate care." But 15 percent of the total U.S. troops in the Persian Gulf, or ten thousand veterans, have illnesses that cannot be diagnosed. By early 1997, the federal government had spent an estimated $80 million trying to determine the causes, which include chemical and/or pesticide exposures, psychological stresses of war, and "a new general mechanism of disease."[6]

"ORDER" IN THE NEW WORLD?

Immediately after the Gulf War, President Bush's popularity was at an all–time high. But in 1992, as the election approached, people were once again worried about rising costs, unemployment, and a recession that had gone on since 1990. Throughout history, voters have been more consistently motivated by economic concerns than any other problems. Bill Clinton and Albert Gore, the Democratic challengers for the White House, knew how important this was to voters. In their campaign headquarters they posted a large banner that read, "It's the Economy, Stupid" to help them focus on the issue that was to bring them victory.

President Clinton came to power at a time when change was the order of the day. As he said in a 1993 speech, "America, to endure, must change . . . change to preserve America's ideals—life, liberty, the pursuit of happiness. Though we march to the music of our time, our mission is timeless." He was reflecting on the need to adapt to the new realities of the twenty-first century. Shifts actually began decades ago, but the effects on the way of life of the average citizen only became apparent and explainable in the last few years of the twentieth century. Some of the most important changes and challenges to society include:

- **THE INFORMATION AGE** It has taken hold and is driven by the personal computer revolution. Connecting via the Internet and other digital networks, individuals, businesses, medical personnel, schools, libraries, and government agencies are rapidly expanding their communications capabilities. As each month goes by, the need to connect to the cyberworld becomes more imperative. Issues of universal access, training, and privacy will have to be resolved.

- **SERVICE-ORIENTED JOBS** More than 75 percent of workers in the United States now have service jobs. Much of this work has to do with information, and it has become more valuable because of computer usage. But the change has meant a very uncomfortable time for many people who worked for years as productive employees in manufacturing plants or in agriculture. Those sectors still are important to the country, but economic growth in the future is dependent on workers who are more highly skilled in technology.

• **MINORITIES AND THE POOR** The increased visibility and demands of minorities, including African Americans, Latinos, Asians, gays/lesbians, the homeless, and the working poor are forcing the dominant white power base of the country to confront issues that have not been adequately addressed in the past. In some cases a conservative backlash has won the day. Welfare reform legislation was passed to eliminate most federal benefits for immigrants—legal as well as illegal—and to limit the length of time anyone can receive welfare services. And as the bulk of immigrants arriving in the U.S. shifts from European countries of origin to Latin America and Asia, there is pressure from many to close U.S. borders even tighter. Affirmative action, once seen as a way to balance inequities in education and the work force, is also facing increased opposition.

• **A GLOBAL ECONOMY** The world continues to grow smaller in terms of communication and business, creating a true global economy. By connecting to worldwide networks, old allies and enemies alike are able to compete. Trade agreements and participation in critical trade organizations have become priorities for U.S. administrations as they attempt to keep U.S. interests paramount in the international markets. Trade missions have become a part of foreign policy.

• **ENVIRONMENTAL ISSUES** The environment continues to receive low priority everywhere on earth, even though scientific evidence shows that crises in air, water, and land use will be more frequent and more severe. The need for Third World countries to quickly modernize to become part of the global marketplace puts even more pressure on the earth's resources. Should these countries be held to a higher standard of environmental responsibility than the advanced industrialized nations? This question is at the heart of the discussion on how to meet the challenge of conserving the world's resources so they will be available for future generations.

In every case, people today are finding it necessary to adapt quickly to the changes around them. For many this is a time of great uncertainty, but for others it opens up new possibilities. The same is true of government as it tries to meet the great challenges posed by technology and the changing geopolitical scene.

With the end of communism as a threat to world democratic societies, the well-defined "enemy" and the driving force behind so much of U.S. government policy simply dissolved, too. In the vacuum that has resulted, the United States has sought to redefine its role on the world stage. As Joseph S. Nye Jr., assistant secretary of defense for international security affairs, wrote:

> Regional balance of power conflicts like the Persian Gulf War are more probable than world wars and could have wide and lasting regional or global implications, although they are less likely than in the past to [bring about] direct military clashes between the great powers.
>
> . . . American leadership is a key factor in limiting the frequency and destructiveness of . . . conflicts. This does not mean that the United States could or should get involved in every potential or ongoing conflict . . . the nation cannot afford the military, economic, and political costs of being a global policeman. Instead, where it has important interests, the United States must continue to aspire to a role more like the sheriff of the posse, enabling international coalitions to pursue interests that it shares whether or not the United States itself supplies the bulk of the military forces involved.[7]

Changes on the political landscape have led to many out-breaks of violence around the world. Some of the conflicts stem from issues and hatreds so old and entrenched that they seem impossible to resolve. Yet some world leaders are trying to go beyond the concept of meeting violence with even greater violence.

One example is Jimmy Carter, former president of the United States and a respected world statesman. Since the late 1980s, he has visited hot spots around the globe as an independent mediator. President Carter believes that "peace is everyone's job," and that is the mission of the Carter Center in Georgia. In an article for the *New York Times* on May 21, 1995, he points out that frequently people in poor countries fight "not only for freedom and self-respect, but also for food and firewood." In his view, one effective "route to peace is through unofficial contacts." Carter advocates working with all types of groups in such activities as "planting wheat or millet, immunizing children, building homes." While carrying out such work, he writes,

> it is natural to cooperate with everyone—government officials, revolutionaries, religious groups, expatriates and other foreigners. We discuss fertilizer, seed, vaccines, roofing materials, pickup trucks and bicycles—and explore common ground on which a peace agreement might be built.
>
> Unfortunately, many government officials resist the involvement of private citizens because to accept outside help is, for some, an admission of failure . . . . But there are many times when officials will not or cannot establish contact with both sides in a conflict. Destruction and suffering continue even as the warring parties search for trusted, neutral mediators. That is why conflict resolution, using every possible means—negotiation, mediation and the holding of democratic elections—is a major priority for me.[8]

One can only hope that such peaceful conflict resolution also becomes a priority for many other leaders and individual citizens worldwide. Perhaps then there will be no need to write additional chapters on what happens "after the shooting stops."

SOURCE NOTES

CHAPTER 1

1. Francis H. Brooke, *A Family Narrative: Being the Reminiscences of a Revolutionary Officer* (Richmond, VA: Macfarlane & Fergusson, 1849; reprinted by the *New York Times* and Arno Press, 1971), 102.
2. Robert C. Bray and Paul E. Bushnell, eds., *Diary of a Common Soldier in the American Revolution 1775-1783 An Annotated Edition of the Military Journal of Jeremiah Greenman* (DeKalb, Ill: Northern Illinois University Press, 1978), 270.
3. Donald B. Cole, *Handbook of American History* (New York: Harcourt, Brace & World, 1968), 40.
4. Daniel J. Boorstin and Brooks Mather Kelley with Ruth Frankel Boorstin, *A History of the United States*, annotated teacher's edition (Englewood Cliffs, N.J.: Prentice-Hall, 1990), 104.
5. "A Little Rebellion Now and Then Is a Good Thing," letter from Thomas Jefferson to James Madison, *The Early*

America Review (Summer 1996), electronic version, no page number.

6. Quoted in John C. Dann, ed., *The Revolution Remembered: Eyewitness Accounts of the War for Independence* (Chicago: University of Chicago Press, 1980), 28.

7. Constitution of the United States, Article I, Section 8.

8. Quoted in John M. Blum, Bruce Catton, Edmund S. Morgan, Arthur M. Schlesinger Jr., Kenneth M. Stampp, and C. Vann Woodward, *The National Experience, Part One*, second edition (New York: Harcourt, Brace & World, 1968), 132.

CHAPTER 2

1. Quoted in Daniel J. Boorstin and Brooks Mather Kelley with Ruth Frankel Boorstin, *A History of the United States*, annotated teacher's edition (Englewood Cliffs, N.J.: Prentice-Hall, 1990), 188.

2. Ibid., 250.

3. Lillian Schlissel, *Women's Diaries of the Westward Journey* (New York: Schocken Books, 1992), 22–24.

4. Quoted in ibid., 9.

5. Quoted in ibid., 66.

6. Quoted in William Loren Katz, *Eyewitness: A Living Documentary of the African American Contribution to American History*, revised edition (New York: Touchstone/ Simon & Schuster, 1995), 90.

7. Ibid., 91.

8. Quoted in Charles M. Snyder, ed., *Red and White on the New York Frontier: A Struggle for Survival; Insights from the Papers of Erastus Granger, Indian Agent 1807–1819* (Harrison, N.Y.: Harbor Hill Books, 1978), 94–95.

9. Kristian Berg, producer/writer, "Dakota Exile" transcript, KTCA Productions, Twin Cities Public Television, 1995.

10 Ibid.

11. Ibid.

12. Rena Maverick Green, ed., *Memoirs of Mary A. Maverick* (Lincoln, Neb.: University of Nebraska Press, 1989), 25.

13. Ibid., 26.

CHAPTER 3

1. Teresa Griffin Vielé, *Following the Drum* (Lincoln, Neb.: University of Nebraska Press, 1984; originally published New York: Rudd & Carleton, 1858), 241.

2. Quoted in Agatha Young, *The Women and the Crisis: Women of the North in the Civil War* (New York: McDowell, Obolensky, 1959), 13.

3. Thomas A. Bailey with Stephen B. Dobbs, *Voices of America: The Nation's Story in Slogans, Sayings, and Songs* (New York: Free Press/Macmillan, 1976), 79.

4. Eleanor Flexner, *Century of Struggle: The Woman's Rights Movement in the United States* (New York: Atheneum, 1974), 57.

5. Quoted in John M. Blum, Bruce Catton, Edmund S. Morgan, Arthur M. Schlesinger Jr., Kenneth M. Stampp, and C. Vann Woodward, *The National Experience, Part One*, second edition (New York: Harcourt, Brace & World, 1968), 258.

6. Quoted in Flexner, *Century of Struggle*, 26.

7. Quoted in William Loren Katz, *Eyewitness: A Living Documentary of the African American Contribution to American History*, revised edition (New York: Touchstone/Simon & Schuster, 1995), 152–153.

8. Quoted in ibid., 154.

9. Ibid., 138.

10. Quoted in Charles M. Wiltse, *The New Nation: 1800–1845* (New York: Hill and Wang, 1961), 158.

CHAPTER 4

1. Quoted in William Loren Katz, *Eyewitnesss: A Living Documentary of the African American Contribution to American History*, revised edition (New York: Touchstone/Simon & Schuster, 1995), 227.

2. George Haven Putnam, *A Prisoner of War in Virginia 1864–1865* (New York: Knickerbocker Press/G. P. Putnam's Sons, 1912), 103–104.

3. Quoted in ibid., 229.

4. Quoted in John Hope Franklin, *Reconstruction After the Civil War* (Chicago: University of Chicago Press, 1961), 158.

5. Kathleen M. Blee, *Women of the Klan* (Berkeley: University of California Press, 1991), 12–13.

6. Kenneth C. Davis, *Don't Know Much About History* (New York: Crown Publishers, 1990), 215.

7. Quoted in Richard B. Morris and James Woodress, eds., *Voices from America's Past: 2* (New York: E. P. Dutton, 1963), 196.

8. George Brown Tindall, *America: A Narrative History, Volume Two*, second edition (New York: W. W. Norton & Company, 1988), 738.

9. A. A. Hoehling, *After the Guns Fell Silent: A Post-Appomattox Narrative, April 1865–March 1866* (London: Madison Books, 1990), 191.

10. Quoted in Daniel J. Boorstin and Brooks Mather Kelley with Ruth Frankel Boorstin, *A History of the United States*, annotated teacher's edition (Englewood Cliffs, N.J.: Prentice-Hall, 1990), 330.

CHAPTER 5

1. Thomas Wentworth Higgison, William Lloyd Garrison, and George S. Boutwell, "Address to the Colored People of the

United States," *Voice of Missions* (November 1, 1900), on the Internet at http://web.syr.edu/~fjzwick/ail98-35.html

2. Quoted in "The War from a Parlor," on the Internet at http://web.syr.edu/~fjzwick/ail98-35.html

3. Quoted in ibid.

4. Quoted in Walter Lord, *The Good Years from 1900 to the First World War* (New York: Harper & Brothers, 1960), p.40.

5. Quoted in ibid.

6. Quoted in James V. Writer, "Did the Mosquito Do It?" *American History* (February 1997), 51.

7. Quoted in Lord, *The Good Years,* 83.

8. Quoted in Eleanor Flexner, *Century of Struggle: The Woman's Rights Movement in the United States* (New York: Atheneum, 1974), 241.

9. Quoted in George Brown Tindall, *America: A Narrative History, Volume Two* (New York: W. W. Norton & Company, 1988), 957.

10. Mary Van Kleek, "Charities and the Commons," report of the National Consumers' League, Consumers' League of New York City, National and New York Child Labor Committees, and College Settlements Association, January 18, 1908.

CHAPTER 6

1. Quoted in Letters, "A Seaman's Armistice Day Diary," *Detroit Free Press,* (December 5, 1993): 3.

2. Quoted in "Portraits in Time," *U.S. News & World Report* (August 28, 1995), electronic version, no page number.

3. Quoted in "The History We Lived," Special Report, *U.S. News & World Report* (August 28, 1995), electronic version, no page number.

4. Robert Cohen, "'Dear Mrs. Roosevelt': Cries for Help

from the Depression Generation, and the American Youth Crisis of the 1930's," (May 1996), on the Internet at http://newdeal.feri.org/eleanor/cohen.htm

5. Ibid.

6. Ibid.

CHAPTER 7

1. Kenneth C. Davis, *Don't Know Much About History* (New York: Crown Publishers, 1990), 320.

2. George Brown Tindall, *America: A Narrative History, Volume Two* (New York: W. W. Norton & Company, 1988), 1277.

3. Quoted in Tindall, *America: A Narrative History,* 1289.

4. Quoted in "The History We Lived," Special Report, *U.S. News & World Report* (August 28, 1995), electronic version, no page number.

5. Youth Division of Soka Gakkai, compilers, Richard L. Graves, ed., *Cries for Peace Experiences of Japanese Victims of World War II* (Tokyo, Japan: Japan Times, Ltd., 1978), 233–234.

6. Bruce Watson, "We Couldn't Run, So We Hoped We Could Hide," *Smithsonian* (April 1994): 47, 53.

7. David Oliver Relin, "Would You Have Rebuilt Japan?" *Scholastic Update* (September 9, 1988), electronic version, no page number.

8. Warren Christopher, "A Tribute to the Berlin Airlift," transcript, U.S. Department of State Dispatch, September 12, 1994.

9. Walter Schneir, "Cryptic Answers," *The Nation* (August 14, 1995), electronic version, no page number.

10. Quoted in Tindall, *America: A Narrative History,* 1271.

11. Interview with Arthur Gay, January 15, 1997.

12. Melba Patillo Beals, "Warriors Don't Cry," *Cosmopolitan* (July 1994), electronic version, no page number.

CHAPTER 8

1. Martin Luther King Jr., "I Have a Dream" speech delivered at Lincoln Memorial, Washington, D.C., August 28, 1963.
2. Quoted in Barthy Byrd, *Home Front: Women and Vietnam* (Berkeley: Shameless Hussy Press, 1986), 46.
3. George Brown Tindall, *America: A Narrative History, Volume Two*, (New York: W. W. Norton & Company, 1988), 1409.
4. W. D. Ehrhart, "Where All the Vietnam War Warriors Gone," *National Catholic Reporter* (September 9, 1994), electronic version, no page number.
5. Walter A. McDougall, "No Discharge from That War," *Current* (May 1996), electronic version, no page number.
6. Larry Heinemann, "The Wall," *Vietnam—Stories Since the War*, on the Internet at http://www.pbs.org/pov/stories/vietnam/story.html, no date.
7. Bill Kovach, "The Writing on the Wall: One Encounter at the Vietnam Memorial," *Washington Monthly* (June 1994): 52.
8. Quoted in Tindall, *America: A Narrative History*, 1448.
9. "Reagan, Help Resolve the Reagan Debate," on the Internet at http://www.openix.com/~tafflink/Lew7.reagan.html, no date.

CHAPTER 9

1. William Perry, testimony before the Senate Foreign Relations Committee, March 1, 1995.
2. Jackie Olsen, "What Price Victory?" *Family Circle* (September 19, 1995), electronic version, no page number.
3. Philip Shenon, "Changes May Be Needed in Study of Gulf War Syndrome, Scientist Says," *New York Times*

(December 10, 1996), electronic version, no page number.

4. Philip Shenon, "White House Panel Staff Assails Pentagon on Gulf War Veterans," *New York Times* (October 10, 1996), electronic version, no page number.

5. Quoted in John Barry, et al. "A Gulf Cover-Up?" *Newsweek* (November 11, 1996), electronic version, no page number.

6. Bill Clements, "Gulf War Mystery," *American Medical News* (January 6, 1997), electronic version, no page number.

7. Joseph S. Nye, Jr., "Future Wars: Conflicts After the Cold War," *Current* (March-April 1996), electronic version, no page number.

8. Jimmy Carter, "Peace Is Everyone's Job," op-ed article, *New York Times* (May 21, 1995), Carter Center homepage on the Internet at http://www.emory.edu/ CARTER_CENTER/ OPEDS/pc-nyts1.htm

FURTHER READING

Brown, Dee. *The American West*. New York: Scribner's, 1994.

Kenneth C. *Don't Know Much About History*. New York: Crown, 1990.

Gay, Kathlyn and Martin Gay. *Voices From the Past* (series on America's wars). New York: Twenty-First Century Books, 1995, 1996.

Hoehling, A. A. *After the Guns Fell Silent: A Post-Appomattox Narrative April 1865-March 1866*. London: Madison Books, 1990.

Kauffman, Stanley. "Album of Bullet Holes." *American Scholar*, Spring 1996.

Logan, Bob. "More Hungry boys." *Commonweal*, February 25, 1994.

Mazower, Mark. "Children and the Aftermath of War." *History Today*, June 1996.

Means, Russell. *Where White Men Fear to Tread*. New York: St. Martin's Press, 1995.

Miller, Tom. "Remember the Main." *Smithsonian*, February 1998.

Moody, Sid. "Welcome Home to the Cold War." *The American Legion*, September 1995.

Mowat, Farley. *Aftermath: Travels in a Post-War World*. Boulder, Colorado: Roberts Rinehart, 1996.

Murphy, Richard W. *The Nation Reunited: War's Aftermath*. Alexandria, Virginia: Time-Life Books, 1987.

Olson, Tod. "On the Soup Line." *Scholastic Update*, February 23, 1996.

Simpson, Elizabeth. *The Spoils of War: World War II and Its Aftermath*. New York: Abrams, 1997.

"The History We Lived." Special Report, *U.S. News & World Report*, August 28, 1995.

INDEX